# Asian Pies

A collection of pies and tarts
with an Asian twist

Evonne Lyn Lee & Sarah FC Lee

 **Marshall Cavendish** Cuisine

# Acknowledgements

Dreams do come true. Holding this pie book is *déja vu*. It's a fulfilment of a prophetic dream that goes back to 2009. In that vivid dream, I was browsing through the colour proofs of a food-related publication.

This book has been made possible by God; my friendship with Sarah spanning several decades and the continual encouragement of our families, friends and neighbours. Perhaps the best blessings came from total strangers — Jeremy Long who snapped several recipe step-by-step images, Suja Manoj who demonstrated her butter chicken recipe at a dinner gathering and the motorcycle shop owner who gave us a small fridge. Plus the vendor at my neighbourhood morning wet market who willingly emptied a gunny sack needed for the photo shoot.

Heartfelt thanks to friends who shared their recipes, food tasters from Malaysia and Singapore and yet others who chipped in to help — Chuei Mey, Connie Lee, Margaret Phan, Aunt Linda Wee, Robert Low, Klein Tan, Lee Bee Chan, Michelle Tham and Lim Cheng Wan who 'chauffeured' Sarah from Malaysia to Singapore on several occasions.

A big thank you also to Team Marshall Cavendish for the opportunity.

This book is dedicated to our beloved late mothers — Mdm Ninie Lee Kim Hiang and Mdm Hui Sow Chan — for having given us a strong foundation in Asian cooking.

(*from left*): Tucking into home-made pies; Aunt Teo Eng Lin, Maheswari, Jenny Tang and Lim Siew Fong.

3

Editor: Melissa Tham
Designer: Lynn Chin

Photography by Calvin Tan except page 3 by Ho Kim Fa, pages 44, 61, 77, 91 and 110 by Jeremy Long of Jemanci and page 83 by Monica Khor

Copyright © 2016 Marshall Cavendish International (Asia) Private Limited
Recipes © Evonne Lyn Lee and Sarah FC Lee

Published by Marshall Cavendish Cuisine
An imprint of Marshall Cavendish International

Limits of Liability/Disclaimer of Warranty: The Author and Publisher of this book have used their best efforts in preparing this book. The parties make no representation or warranties with respect to the contents of this book and are not responsible for the outcome of any recipe in this book. While the parties have reviewed each recipe carefully, the reader may not always achieve the results desired due to variations in ingredients, cooking temperatures and individual cooking abilities. The parties shall in no event be liable for any loss of profit or any other commercial damage, including but not limited to special, incidental, consequential or other damages.

Other Marshall Cavendish Offices: Marshall Cavendish Corporation. 99 White Plains Road, Tarrytown NY 10591-9001, USA • Marshall Cavendish International (Thailand) Co Ltd. 253 Asoke, 12th Flr, Sukhumvit 21 Road, Klongtoey Nua, Wattana, Bangkok 10110, Thailand • Marshall Cavendish (Malaysia) Sdn Bhd, Times Subang, Lot 46, Subang Hi-Tech Industrial Park, Batu Tiga, 40000 Shah Alam, Selangor Darul Ehsan, Malaysia

Marshall Cavendish is a trademark of Times Publishing Limited

National Library Board, Singapore Cataloguing in Publication Data

Name(s): Lee, Evonne Lyn. | Lee, Sarah F.C, author.
Title: Asian pies : a collection of pies and tarts with an Asian twist / Evonne Lyn Lee & Sarah FC Lee.
Description: Singapore : Marshall Cavendish Cuisine, [2016]
Identifier(s): OCN 945630470 | ISBN 978-981-47-5155-1 (paperback)
Subject(s): LCSH: Pies--Asia. | Pastry--Asia. | Cooking, Asian. | Cookbooks.
Classification: LCC TX773 | DDC 641.8652--dc23

Printed by Times Offset (M) Sdn Bhd

# Contents

# Recipes

# Introduction

Growing up, my co-author Sarah and I were constantly surrounded by the aromas of Asian cooking from our beloved late mothers' kitchens, and this cookbook, *Asian Pies*, stems from the memories that are vivid till today. Here, we present our heirloom recipes for rich curries, flavourful stews and desserts, but adapted as fillings for pies and tarts. By giving the dishes a contemporary twist, we hope they will appeal to the younger generation, connecting them with their culinary heritage and helping to preserve it.

Flexibility underpins the recipes in this book. Should you make the spice pastes from scratch or use ready-made ones? It's your choice. Don't fancy pork? Go ahead and substitute it with chicken. Lack the equipment like pie dishes or tart tins? You can use clay pots, oven-proof Corningware dishes, stainless steel or aluminium tins and trays and even enamelware including traditional tiffin carriers (*tingkat*).

For the pastry required in these recipes, you can use flaky, shortcrust, phyllo or puff pastry. If you prefer puff or phyllo pastry, using the store-bought version will save you the time and effort of making your own. But if you're game to roll up your sleeves and make your own pastry, try the plain, spiced and shortcrust pastry recipes developed by Sarah to complement the Asian pie fillings featured in this book. You could also make your own flaky pastry.

We hope you will enjoy baking the pies and tarts as much as we enjoyed coming up with them.

# Basic Ingredients

Pastry is essentially made with basic ingredients like fat, flour and water. To this, other secondary ingredients are also added to create variations in pastry.

**FATS:** Whether it is butter, margarine, vegetable shortening or lard, fat is an essential ingredient when it comes to pastry making as it acts to coat and separate flour particles. In the process, it creates a pastry texture that is flaky and crumbly. Puff or shortcrust pastry can be made with a single fat (e.g. butter alone) or a combo of fats (butter and shortening). A good pastry needs at least 80% of fat.

**BUTTER** A high fat content of 80% lends pastry tremendous flavour and enhances the overall taste of pies. All-butter pastry is puffy, airy and lighter as compared to one that combines butter with shortening. There are two types of butter sold, unsalted and salted. Opt for unsalted butter which is fresher and has more flavour than the salted version.

Although margarine can be used as a substitute for butter, it is not ideal as it contains 50% fat and 50% water which yields a limp pastry. Pastry margarine, a cheaper alternative to butter, was formulated for the industrial production of *viennoiserie* that yields a fluffy texture but has lacklustre flavour. Pastry margarine is 100% fat and is preferred by chefs because it is easier to handle given its wider temperature range and good structure.

**VEGETABLE SHORTENING** is also 100 % fat, solidified at room temperature. Shortening has a higher melting point (refers to the temperature at which solid fat melts) than butter. This means it can withstand higher temperature and does not melt so fast, so it is easier to work with. As shortening is flavourless, it is usually combined with butter for flavour.

TIP A rule of thumb in butter-flour pastry mixture is that the fat should not exceed 50% of the quantity of flour. Hot and humid weather may pose a challenge when working with pastry. When butter begins to melt during the rolling or shaping process, the pastry becomes oily and sticky. If making pastry by hand, cut the butter into smaller cubes with a knife or pastry blender. Continue with the cutting motion to slow down gluten development, adding the water in the last few minutes. Then bring it all together into a dough with your hands as quickly as possible. Generally, it is better to make pastry when the weather is cooler — in the evenings, at night, and early morning.

**EGGS** We used commercial eggs which include both brown and white free-range (*kampung*) eggs, each weighing between 60–65 g (2$\frac{1}{4}$–2$\frac{1}{2}$ oz). The egg acts as a gelling agent to bind pastry and ingredients together so that it holds its shape. It also gives pastry flavour apart from imparting a light to golden yellow hue when baked.

**SALT** is all-important in making pies. This vital ingredient helps to make the dough more elastic as it interacts with flour. When there is enough salt, the taste of both the pastry and filling come through.

**SUGAR** is often added to sweet shortcrust pastry to give it a good crisp. It inhibits gluten development which results in a tender pastry that crisps up as sugar caramelises during baking.

**FLOUR** A tender delicious pastry requires a good balance of protein and starch. Understanding the role of protein in pastry is helpful — it acts as the building block to lend structure to baked goods. Pastry flour which has between 8–10% of protein content and enough elasticity to hold buttery layers together makes it ideal for pie crusts, croissants and puff pastries. Too much protein produces a hard pastry whereas too little causes the pastry to be brittle. Normal wheat or plain or all-purpose flour has a protein content of 10–12% and works well for most pies.

**SELF-RAISING FLOUR** has baking powder and salt added to it. For freshness, always use it by the expiry date as the baking powder loses its efficacy over time. If you run out of self-raising flour, make a fresh batch by mixing 1$\frac{1}{4}$ teaspoon of baking powder and $\frac{1}{4}$ teaspoon of salt to 130 g (4$\frac{3}{4}$ oz) of plain flour.

**WHOLEWHEAT (*ATTA*)** We used finely ground wholewheat (*atta*) which has more fibre than all-purpose flour. It does not absorb liquid as fast as plain flour owing to its texture. Allow it to rest for 30 minutes at room temperature before rolling.

# 10 Hot Tips

1. The grain texture of plain/all-purpose or normal wheat flour varies, depending on the country of origin. This will affect the absorbency of liquid (water, egg) added to form a dough. Always use chilled water when making shortcrust pastry so that the fat will not soften or melt. Start with 1 tablespoon, adding more until you get a soft and malleable dough.

2. If using a food processor to make dough, blend the dry ingredients, then add the fat and pulse until the mixture resembles breadcrumbs. Add water 1 tablespoon at a time to form a soft and pliable dough.

3. To roll out dough, use silicon baking sheets to prevent it from sticking to the rolling pin. Place the dough between two sheets, then gently roll the pin over the top sheet. Plastic sheets cut out to A3 size are good alternatives as they can be discarded after baking.

4. When rolling out store-bought block puff or shortcrust pastry, do not roll it thinner than 5 mm ($^1/_5$ in) as the pastry will not rise to airy lightness.

5. Always chill shortcrust pastry in the fridge until firm before rolling and even after rolling before baking. This allows the gluten (that gives elasticity) in the flour to relax and prevents the pastry from shrinking while baking. For blast chilling, putting the pastry-lined dishes/cases in the freezer cuts the resting time by half.

6. Always ensure filling has cooled down before spooning it into pie dishes/cases. If it is still hot, it may melt the bottom pastry. It also becomes difficult to lay the top pastry over the filling. Chill the filling in the refrigerator overnight for the sauce to thicken. This makes it easier to handle when spooning the filling over a pastry base. Do not freeze the filling as it secretes water while it thaws during the baking process, causing the bottom pastry to become soggy.

7. For moist fillings like curries, mark the top pastry with a cross to create steam holes for steam to escape during baking. Do not make more than three steam holes or pastry will not rise well.

8. For maximum flavours in curry fillings cooked with a *rempah*, use freshly ground spices. To draw out the aromas, toast whole spices before grinding them in a spice grinders.

9. Cooked curry is generally oily. Allow filling to cool down. To remove the oil, spread a piece of greaseproof paper over the filling, gently push the oil to the side of the saucepan, scrunching the paper at the same time to soak up the excess liquid fat. Discard. The paper acts like an oil blotter. Chill overnight and discard the solidified fat sitting on top of the filling.

10. For double-crusted pies, preheat baking trays at the same time as the oven. Place the pie onto the heated tray. This will kick start the cooking of the bottom pastry. Position the rack closer to the bottom heat.

# Baking Terms

Baking blind

### BAKING BLIND

Blind baking is a process to partially or fully cook the pastry base before filling is added. After lining a pan with the bottom crust, prick the base with a fork to stop it from buckling while baking. Lay a piece of greaseproof paper 7.5 cm (3 in) larger than the pie dish/case over the pastry base and weigh it down with ceramic pastry/baking beads or dried beans/rice/legumes. Bake in a preheated oven at 200°C (400°F) for 15 minutes until the pastry is set. Remove weights and paper, wait 5 minutes, then brush pastry with lightly beaten egg white to seal the pastry. This prevents it from getting soggy from runny fillings like curries, chocolate and custard. Return to the oven to bake for a further 5 minutes until golden brown. Cool completely before using.

TIP To make this process easier, freeze pastry cases for 15–20 minutes until firm, then transfer directly from the freezer to a preheated oven and bake as directed in the recipe.

Rolling out pastry

### ROLLING PASTRY

Dust kitchen/working top with some flour. Roll out the pastry outwards, starting from the centre. This strengthens the gluten without making the dough tough. Rotate it at quarter turns to ensure a thin and even pastry. For square-based pies/tarts, rotate it at 90 degrees while rolling out. To keep it to the desired shape, pat in the edges with your fingers.

TIP Always dust some flour on the work surface and not the pastry to prevent it from drying out.

### DOUBLE-CRUST

This refers to pies with bottom and top crusts. Divide pastry dough into half. Roll out one portion to 3 mm ($^1/_8$ in) thickness and 5 cm (2 in) larger than the pie dish/case. Meanwhile, cover remaining dough with a moistened tea towel or wrap in cling film. To lift up the rolled pastry, wrap it around a rolling pin. Gently unroll it into the base of a pie dish, taking care not to stretch the dough. Trim excess dough. Add the filling, roll out the remaining dough 2–5 cm ($^3/_4$–2 in) larger than the edge of the pie dish to cover the pie. Press edges together to seal. Trim excess dough before glazing pie tops.

Lining Pie Dish

Trimming Pastry

Docking

## LINING PIE/TART TINS

Lift up the rolled-out pastry on the rolling pin, wrapping it round loosely if necessary, then hold it over the centre of the pie dish and unroll it into the dish. Lightly press it into the corners with your fingertips, making sure you do not stretch the pastry. Trim excess dough with a sharp knife or, if you are using a dish without a rim, such as a flan tin, just run the rolling pin lightly over the top to cut off the excess. Chill for 10–15 minutes before filling or baking blind; this helps prevent shrinkage in a hot oven.

## TRIMMING PASTRY

After covering the filling with dough, lift up the pie in one hand and using a knife at an angle, cut off excess dough along the entire edge. Reserve trimmings to decorate pie tops. Glaze with an egg wash and make steam holes before baking.

## DOCKING

A fork is used to dock or prick the pastry base before blind-baking it. Docking allows the steam formed during baking to escape so that the pastry stays flat.

Crimping pastry with a spoon      Crimping pastry with a fork      Crimping pastry using thumb and fingers

## CRIMPING PASTRY – SOME BASIC METHODS

There are multiple ways to crimp the edges of pies and tarts. Decorative patterns enhance the visual appeal of baked pastries. The possibilities are endless and this is where pie baking becomes fun.

**FORK** Leave a slight overhang of pastry along the entire rim of the dish, using the back of a fork, lightly press evenly around the edge. **SPOON** Using a small teaspoon facing down, press lightly along the rim. **WEAVE** Trim the pastry to the exact width of the rim. Take a kitchen scissors, snip at 1 cm (½ in) intervals all the way around the rim. Fold alternate tabs of dough inwards. **RUFFLED** Trim pastry with a 1 cm (½ in) overhang all around; place the thumb inside the pie edge, with the thumb and index of the other hand, gently press the dough around the thumb. **ZIG-ZAG** With rims wider than 1 cm (½ in), make small cuts at an angle with a sharp kitchen scissors all around the pie. Fold each tab over to form a triangle. **PEARLS** Press a string of cleaned pearls into the dough along the rim. **BRAIDED** Braid three 1 cm (½ in) strips together, lay it along the pie rim pinching the ends together to close it up. **CORKSCREW** Press the screw into the dough along the rim. **CUT-OUT EDGES** Trim pastry to the exact width of pie rim, lightly moisten with water. Press cut-outs of different designs, overlapping slightly as they are laid along the rim. **ROPE** Twist two long thin sausage-shaped dough together to form a rope. Press into position along the moistened edge of the pie case.

At all times, the dough should rest directly on the pie rim. Tuck excess dough under for a smooth edge.

TIP After crimping, press down along the inside of the pie to puncture any air bubbles.

Decorating pie tops with pleats    Decorating pies with alphabet cut-outs    Decorating pies using a lattice cutter

## DECORATING PIES WITH PASTRY TRIMMINGS

Put pastry scraps to good use by decorating pie tops using trimmings after crimping. Given the myriad of cookie/pastry cutters, the range of creative cut-outs is limited only by one's imagination.

## GLAZING

Brushing a pie with a liquid glaze is the final step before baking. It seals any tears in the pastry and adds a sheen. There are different glazes — whole eggs, egg white, milk and water — each giving different appearances when baked. Lightly beaten whole egg yields pastry with a rich, yellow hue. **Egg yolks** only give a deep golden hue whereas **egg whites** give pies a clean shiny finish. Sweet shortcrust usually made with golden egg yolks tends to look more yellow. A **milk glaze** gives a brown and matte finish. **Water glaze** gives a clean and sheer look when baked. Always glaze thinly and evenly and before decorating pies with pastry cut-outs. For a deeper golden crust, add a double-coating of glaze, allowing the first coat to dry out before brushing on the second coat.

## STEAM HOLES

As the pie bakes, steam builds up in the filling which can cause the pastry to become soggy. To prevent this, make ripped holes rather than neatly cut holes to release steam during baking. Some bakers use a porcelain pie funnel to channel the steam out much like a chimney.

Opening up lattice design                  Placing lattice design over pie

## PLANNING A PIE PARTY

Here's a general guide when deciding on quantity, size of the pie and number of people to serve when planning a pie party. For ease of reference, pies in this cookbook are broadly categorised into 3 sizes: snack (bite size), personal (individual, based on an average male's appetite) and family. Puff pastry used in this cookbook is store-bought and come in 24-cm ($9^1/_2$-in) square sheets.

| No | Pie Size | No. of Servings | Shortcrust Pastry | Mashed Potato | Filling |
|----|----------|-----------------|-------------------|---------------|---------|
| 1 | Snack (7 x 2.5 cm) ($2^4/_5$ x 1 in) | 1 serving | Top and bottom crust each 25–27 g (1 oz) | 40 g ($1^1/_4$ oz) | 45 g ($1^1/_2$ oz) |
| 2 | Personal 10 cm (4 in) | 1 serving | Top and bottom crust each 83–85 g (3 oz) | 70 g | 125–130 g ($4^1/_2$ oz) |
| 3 | Family 20 cm (8 in) | 4–5 servings | Top and bottom crust each 260–265 g ($9^1/_{10}$ oz) | 500 g (1 lb $1^1/_2$ oz) | 255–260 g ($9^1/_{10}$ oz) |

# Baking Tools

**Baking Trays/Sheets Parchment Paper ❶ Silicon Baking Mats/Sheets**

Baking trays/sheets are useful when baking a large number of savoury and sweet goods that include pies, tarts, galettes, hand pies, turnovers and puffs. Material includes aluminium, carbon steel and stainless steel. They can be lined with silicon baking mats/sheets or parchment (greaseproof paper) to catch spillage (liquid oozing out from pies) making it easy to clean the trays.

**❷ Cookie Cutters**

Embellishing pie tops and tarts with cut-outs gives the impression of embossed designs, enhancing their visual appeal and makes them enticing. Cookie cutters which are moulds to stamp or cut out pastry dough are available in a wide range of sizes, materials (plastic, aluminium, stainless steel or even copper) and designs (from alphabets, animals, flowers to leaves and even plain round or square ones). The wide variety of shapes and designs enable you to personalise a pie top for a loved one or special occasion.

**❸ Fork, Knives (❹ Butter/ ❺ Palette/Serrated) ❻ Spoons (Slotted) ❼ Pastry Brush**

These tools are the most used in making pies. A fork is useful in two ways — to prick the base of a pie dough before blind-baking and to crimp pies to seal the edges. This conceals the filling while it cooks. When crimping a pie, excess dough is trimmed using a butter knife and is also used to cut pastry strips to embellish pie tops.

A palette knife is a metal spatula with rounded blades; it is particularly useful for smoothing and levelling pie fillings as well as to remove baked goods from baking sheets before transferring to a cooling/wire rack. The serrated knife, on the other hand, is ideal for cutting chunky pies and tarts in a sawing motion without the crust cracking. To scoop filling into a pie dough, use a slotted spoon.

A pastry brush is primarily used to glaze pie tops with water or egg wash before baking and for brushing fruit tarts with jam glazes. Choose brushes with natural bristles and wooden handles as opposed to nylon bristles.

**❽ Lattice Cutter**

It comprises a series of wheels to cut a patterned look that resembles a fish net. The cutter is rolled over a flat piece of dough. It is then lifted and laid over the filling. With the hands, the dough is gently stretched outwards, starting from the centre to ease it open to produce a lattice design.

**Mixing Bowls, Measuring Jug/ ❾ Measuring Cups/Spoons**

Mixing bowls which come in different sizes and materials (glass, stainless steel, plastic, wooden) have multi-purposes — apart from blending and mixing different ingredients together, they are good for marinating meat and also serve as receptacles to cool down fillings. Pots can also be used as mixing bowls. To measure dry and liquid ingredients, a measuring jug, cups of varying sizes ($1/4$, $1/2$, $1/3$ and 1 cup) and spoons ($1/4$, $1/2$, full teaspoon, full tablespoon) are required.

**Oven**

A good oven is essential in turning out golden brown pies and tarts. Oven temperatures in this book are based on a conventional oven. If using fan-forced (convection) mode, reduce the temperature by 20°C (35.6°F). Some ovens may heat up faster than others, depending on the brand, so getting to know your home oven is important to ensure successful baking. It is important to preheat the oven at least 10–15 minutes before baking. Do not open the oven door regularly throughout the baking process as it causes temperatures to dip and leads to an uneven browning of the pies.

### Pastry Board/Sheets
A marble pastry board is most suitable for mixing dough and rolling out pastry. This is because marble remains cool to the touch in tropical climates. Kitchen top surfaces that have smooth, cool surfaces e.g. granite, stainless steel, ceramic tiles, soapstone and even concrete are also suitable. Good alternatives are a marble table top or loose pieces of ceramic tiles.

### Pastry Blender
This is a useful tool not only to cut fat (butter and/or shortening) into the flour but also for blending and incorporating softer ingredients like yoghurt and citrus zest into the pie dough. It is handy for those whose hands tend to be warm.

### ⑩ Pie Dishes (Glass/Ceramics, Enamel/Porcelain/Disposable Aluminium/Paper) ⑪ Tins (Tranche/Loose-Bottomed, Round/Square) ⑫ Ramekin, Flan
The Asian kitchen is filled with a wide array of receptacles that make suitable pie dishes. Professional ones come in different shapes and sizes, with many variations — loose-bottoms, clipped sides, scalloped edges, heart-shaped etc. They are made of common material like stainless steel, silicone, ceramic and glass. In addition, disposable aluminium trays and even paper ones are now available at specialist baking supply shops. To ascertain the capacity of a pie dish, fill it up with water. Use a measuring cup to find out how much cups it can hold. The number of cups will be equivalent to how much filling a pie dish can hold.

### ⑬ Piping Nozzles ⑭ Piping Bags
Piping bags are filled with whipped cream to pipe toppings onto pie tops. Disposable piping bags are best and they come in different sizes. Nozzles, plain or fluted, also come in different sizes.

### ⑮ Rolling Pin
The most common are wooden pins, although marble, which used to be popular, is now rare. Some have handles which can either be fixed or made from a single piece of wood, while others without handles are shaped like batons.

### Ruler/Measuring Tape
A metal ruler or measuring tape is good for cutting pastry to the desired size as well as for measuring the size (length, width and depth) of a tin or tray.

### ⑯ Spatula/Scraper
References to spatula or scraper are used interchangeably. These are handy for smoothing surfaces of fillings of pies and tarts. Bowl scrapers made of plastic or silicone are great for removing batter/filling from mixing bowls whereas metal scrapers are used to cut, scrape dough from a work top or to transfer delicate goods onto baking trays or onto serving plates.

### ⑰ Wire Rack/Cooling Rack
A wire rack is good way to cool baked goods as it allows air to circulate around them to speed up the cooling process.

### ⑱ Whisk
A balloon whisk is excellent for whisking sauces, cream fillings and egg washes. A pair of chopsticks or a large fork can also do the job.

# Baking Techniques

## USING STORE-BOUGHT PASTRY

Good quality ready-made pastry (puff, shortcrust and phyllo) are sold chilled or frozen in sheets or blocks in major supermarkets. Resting periods differ for each type of pastry and how it is packed (whether rolled, block or sheets), so please do check and follow the instructions on the pack. For **puff**, it is made with either margarine or butter, rolled or in sheets of varying sizes ranging from 230 g–1 kg (8–2 lb 3 oz). Butter-only puff pastry yields an unmistakably delicious butter flavour with a light puffy texture. However, it can be oily when over-handled in tropical weather. Take out the required number of sheets a few minutes before lining the dishes/cases. If the pastry sheets get too soft, it is hard to shape. If this happens, chill until firm.

Shortcrust pastry, however, needs resting in the refrigerator for 30 minutes before using or it may crack if not properly handled. **Phyllo** needs to be brought to room temperature after standing 1–2 hours. However, it can become dry, brittle and break easily, so keep it covered under a damp dish towel. Before baking, phyllo pastry needs to be gently brushed with a flavoursome oil (e.g. peanut) or melted salted butter. When brushing phyllo, always brush the edges first to prevent it from curling and cracking.

## STORING AND FREEZING PASTRY

Freshly-made pastry can be kept chilled in the fridge for 2–3 days until the day of baking. Wrap the dough in cling film, store in a ziplock bag or airtight container. It can be frozen for up to a month. Thaw overnight in the fridge and stand at room temperature until it softens, approximately 30–45 minutes depending on the weather. When baking with phyllo and puff, it is best to bake them fresh and consume on the same day as reheating would cause them to shrink and dry up. Do not re-freeze thawed pastry.

## PRE-BAKING PASTRY CASES

To save time, puff and shortcrust pastry cases can be baked up to 2 days ahead and cooled before freezing. Store in airtight containers until ready to use. Ready-made pastry cases can be frozen for up to a month. For puff pastry cases, it is best to consume them on the same day. On baking day, remove cases from the freezer, spoon the filling into them and proceed to bake as per the recipe. For speed and convenience, pre-baked pastry cases — shortcrust, puff, phyllo — in different sizes are available in supermarkets and baking supply shops.

## REMOVING BAKED GOODS FROM LOOSE-BOT-TOMED PANS

After the pie/tart has cooled slightly, place the whole tray onto a glass or tin can and let the ring slide down. Allow pie to cool 5–10 more minutes before slowly easing the pies from the base onto a serving plate using a palette knife.

## TROUBLE-SHOOTING

### When Pastry Turns Sticky While Rolling Out

When too much liquid is added to the dough while mixing, it becomes wet and sticky. To get it pliable again, add a bit of flour at a time, kneading it into the dough until it comes away clean from your fingers. Hot temperatures or those with warm hands can also cause the dough to soften too quickly. When it happens, sprinkle some flour on the dough.

### When Pastry Cracks During Baking

When pastry starts to buckle or bubble during blind baking, that is because there is trapped air. Remove from the oven, prick the pastry with a fork and return it to baking. However, if the pastry cracks during baking, remove from the oven, brush with lightly beaten egg white and bake another 3–4 minutes. This seals up the crack and stops the filling from leaking. If the crack is large, patch it with raw dough, then give it an egg wash before baking it again till it is done.

### Preventing Soggy Bottom Pastry

For savoury pies, sprinkle a thin layer of breadcrumbs over the pastry base to absorb any liquid that oozes during baking. This is particularly true with seafood (crabmeat, fish, prawns and scallops) as they shrink during baking and release water, so pre-cooking it before baking is best. Always use fresh seafood and not frozen. For sweet shortcrust pastry cases, brush the base with lightly beaten egg white, then return to oven and bake for another few minutes until light brown. This stops creamy fillings from seeping into the pastry and making it soggy. To prevent soggy bottom crusts in pies with curry fillings, line sliced potatoes over the chilled pastry base before adding the filling. This helps to absorb any liquid that oozes from the filling during baking. Alternatively, use a specialised baking tray where the base and sides have perforated holes. If not available, buy 10 cm (4 in) disposable paper cases punctured with holes at a major baking supply store.

### Sweet Shortcrust Over-browning

Monitor the baking of sweet shortcrust towards the last 15–20 minutes as it can burn quickly and cause the crust to taste bitter owing to the added sugar in the pastry. If it has turned golden brown before the filling is cooked, cover the pie with aluminium foil to stop it from over-browning.

### When Puff Pastry Sweats

During hot tropical weather, do not leave puff pastry at room temperature beyond 30 minutes or it will start to 'sweat' — i.e. ooze with oil. When this happens, wrap with cling film and chill it in the fridge till firm. Those with warm hands need to be swift when working with puff pastry.

TIP Wash your hands under cold running water and pat dry before handling puff pastry.

# Basic Recipes

Shortcrust pastry can be made up to 2 days in advance. Wrap well in cling film and chill until ready to use. Stand at room temperature for 45 minutes (depending on the weather) until softened slightly before rolling it out.

## Plain Shortcrust

350 (12 oz) plain (all-purpose) flour

110 g (4 oz) butter, diced into 1-cm ($\frac{1}{2}$-in) cubes

60 g ($2\frac{1}{4}$ oz) vegetable shortening

60–120 ml (2–4 fl oz / $\frac{1}{4}$– $\frac{1}{2}$ cup) chilled water

1. Sieve flour in a medium mixing bowl. Rub butter and vegetable shortening into the flour until mixture resembles breadcrumbs.

2. Add chilled water, a tablespoon at a time, until the mixture forms a dough. Wrap with cling film and refrigerate for at least 30 minutes. Discard any excess water.

3. Remove the pastry from the fridge. Using a rolling pin, roll it out to 3 mm ($\frac{1}{8}$ in) thickness. Line the base of the dish with one sheet of pastry. Trim excess dough and set aside.

   *Note:* Generally suitable for savoury pies, hand pies and turnovers, regardless of whether they are single or double-crusted.

## Atta (wholewheat) Shortcrust

350 (12 oz) fine wholewheat (*atta*) flour

$\frac{1}{2}$ tsp salt

100 g ($3\frac{1}{2}$ oz) butter, diced into 1-cm ($\frac{1}{2}$-in) cubes

70 g ($2\frac{1}{2}$ oz) vegetable shortening

75 ml (2.5 fl oz / $\frac{1}{4}$ cup) chilled water

1. Sift wholewheat flour in a large mixing bowl. Add salt, butter and vegetable shortening and mix well.

2. Lightly knead with your fingers until mixture resembles breadcrumbs. Add water, a bit at a time, while kneading until it forms a dough. Dough is ready when it does not stick to your fingers.

3. Shape dough into a disc. Wrap with cling film and chill in the fridge for 30 minutes. This allows the gluten in the flour to relax which yields a tender and pliable dough.

   *Note:* Suitable for pot pies especially robust curries or stews with a thick gravy.

## Yoghurt Shortcrust

170 g (6 oz) plain (all-purpose) flour

100 g ($3\frac{1}{2}$ oz) butter, diced into 1-cm ($\frac{1}{2}$-in) cubes

2 tsp sugar

1 egg yolk

50 g ($1\frac{2}{3}$ oz) natural yoghurt

a pinch of salt

1. Place flour, butter and sugar in a food processor and pulse until mixture resembles breadcrumbs.

2. Add egg yolk, natural yoghurt and salt. Continue to pulse until the mixture forms a dough. Shape dough into a disc, wrap with cling film and chill in the fridge for 30 minutes.

   *Note:* Yoghurt shortcrust pastry texture is softer than other shortcrust versions in this cookbook. If the dough is still sticky, add a little more flour and knead until smooth. Ideal for pie fillings which are drier and do not have too much gravy, e.g. mutton *karipap* and sambal dried prawn and *petai* hand pies.

## Five-spice Shortcrust

350 (12 oz) plain (all-purpose) flour

1½ tsp five-spice powder

170 g (6 oz) butter, diced into
  1-cm (½-in) cubes

5 Tbsp water, at room temperature

1. In a medium mixing bowl, sift flour and five-spice powder together. Rub butter into flour mixture until the mixture resembles breadcrumbs. If using a food processor, pulse together until mixture becomes breadcrumbs.

2. Add water, a tablespoon at a time, until it forms a dough.

3. Flatten into a disc and wrap with cling film. Chill in the fridge for 30 minutes before using.

## Cumin Shortcrust

100 g (3½ oz) fine wholewheat (*atta*) flour

150 g (5 oz) plain (all-purpose) flour

½ tsp cumin, whole

a pinch of salt

100 g (4 oz) butter, diced into
  1-cm (½-in) cubes

25 g (⅘ oz) vegetable shortening

3–5 Tbsp chilled water

1. Sift both flours and cumin together in a medium mixing bowl. If mixing by hand, add the salt, butter and shortening. Rub the fat into the mixture with your fingers until it resembles breadcrumbs.

2. If using a food processor, pulse all the ingredients together except water until it becomes breadcrumbs. Transfer contents to a medium mixing bowl.

3. Add water, a tablespoon at a time, until mixture forms a dough. Flatten into a disc and wrap with cling film. Chill in the fridge for 30 minutes before using.

*Note: This is ideal for curries or stews cooked with spices. Cumin, owing to its small size is used whole which makes rolling out easy. However, for harder spices like cinnamon, coriander, fennel, nutmeg and cardamom, use the powder form. As spices are intense, one teaspoon of ground spice suffices, except for cardamom, half the quantity.*

## Sweet Pastry

430 g (15 oz) flour

50 g (1⅔ oz) icing sugar

185 g (6½ oz) cold butter, diced
  into 1-cm (½-in) cubes

2 egg yolks

2–3 Tbsp chilled water

1. Place flour, icing sugar, cold butter and egg yolks in a deep mixing bowl. Using your fingers, rub in butter until it resembles breadcrumbs. Alternatively, you can also pulse all the ingredients together in a food processor.

2. Add water, a little at a time, and knead until the dough does not stick to your fingers. If using a food processor, transfer contents to a medium mixing bowl. Mix until it forms a dough. Flatten into a disc and chill in the fridge for 30 minutes before using.

*Note: Suitable for any sweet fruit pies.*

## Chocolate Pastry

20 cm (8 in) square/round tart tin

20 tartlet cases (1 tablespoon capacity)

150 g (5 oz) fine wholemeal (*atta*) flour,
  sifted

2 Tbsp extra dark cocoa powder, sifted

1 Tbsp brown sugar

2 Tbsp castor sugar

100 g (3½ oz) butter, diced into 1-cm (½-in) cubes

1. Place wholewheat flour, cocoa powder, brown sugar, castor sugar and butter into a food processor. Pulse until well combined and it forms a dough.

2. Wrap with cling film and chill for 20 minutes before blind baking at 180°C (350°F) for 12–15 minutes.

*Note: Options for upside down banana tart and chocolate and chilli tart.*

# Quick Step Flaky Pastry

225 g (8 oz) plain (all-purpose) flour +
  4 Tbsp for dusting and rolling

3/4 tsp salt

200 g (7 oz) butter, semi-frozen
  and cut into cubes

125 ml (4 fl oz / 1/2 cup) light sour
  cream or yoghurt, chilled

1. Place flour, salt and butter in a food processor. Pulse until butter breaks into pea-size pieces.

2. Add sour cream or yoghurt and mix with a pastry scraper or rubber spatula. Transfer onto a lightly floured silicon baking sheet. Using your hands, gently bring it together to form a rough dough. At this stage, the mixture is crumbly and loose. Shape and roll dough into a cylinder. Using your finger tips, work quickly to pat dough into a square. You will still see the butter and bits of the cream in the mixture. Wrap with cling film and chill in the freezer for 45 minutes or until firm.

3. Sandwich the dough between two silicon baking sheets or thick plastic sheets measuring 45 x 25 cm (18 x 10 in). Roll it out to a 40 x 20 cm (16 x 8 in) rectangle, then roll it up like a Swiss roll. Wrap and chill the dough in the freezer for 45 minutes or until firm.

4. Begin the double-book fold — this is a process where the folding process is repeated up to four x four times. This helps to build layers in the pastry. Starting from the left, fold a quarter-way inwards, towards the centre. Do the same for the right flap until both the long edges meet in the centre. It should look like a double page of a book.

5. Fold both sides towards each other, with the shorter end facing you. Wrap and chill in the freezer for 45 minutes.

6. Unwrap the chilled dough. Place at a right angle between two silicon baking sheets. Roll it out to a rectangle with the same measurement as in Step 3. Wrap and chill for 30 minutes.

7. Repeat the double-book step another two more times.

8. After the final fold, allow the dough to rest in the refrigerator for at least 2 hours before baking. The dough can be frozen for up to two weeks.

*Note:* If the butter starts to melt and seep through the pastry, sprinkle the baking sheet, not the dough, with a little flour.

# Sambal Tumis (Fried Chilli Paste)

Makes 860 g (1 3/4 lb)

600 g (1 lb 5 1/3 oz) store-bought
  ground chilli

4 large onions, peeled and
  coarsely chopped

1 1/2 heads garlic, peeled and
  coarsely chopped

3 Tbsp toasted shrimp paste (*belacan*)
  or 3 1/2 Tbsp *belacan* powder

4 Tbsp tamarind pulp (*asam jawa*)*
  diluted in 250 ml (8 fl oz / 1 cup) water

1 tsp salt

140 g (5 oz) sugar + more to taste

125 ml (4 fl oz / 1/2 cup) oil +
  more if needed

1. Place all ingredients except the oil in a food processor and grind until fine. Transfer the mixture to a medium mixing bowl.

2. Heat oil in a wok or medium saucepan over medium heat. Add ground ingredients and sauté until it is aromatic and becomes a thick paste. Add the tamarind, salt and sugar to taste.

3. Allow sambal *tumis* to cool and store in a jar. Keep paste refrigerated after opening.

# Laksa Rempah

Makes 310 g (11 oz)

4 Tbsp oil

2 tsp tamarind water

1 1/2 tsp palm sugar

a pinch of salt

**REMPAH**

4 Tbsp fried chilli paste (sambal *tumis*)

4 cloves garlic, peeled and diced

3 onions, peeled and diced

30 g dried shrimps, soaked for 10 minutes

2 lemongrass (*serai*), white portion,
  thickly sliced

4 candlenuts (*buah keras*), roughly chopped

1 tsp shrimp paste (*belacan*), dry toasted

2 tsp coriander, dry toasted then finely ground

Double thumb-size galangal (*lengkuas*),
  peeled and diced

Thumb-size turmeric (*kunyit*), peeled
  and diced

1 kaffir lime rind (*kulit limau purut*), sliced

1 torch ginger bud, rough outer leaves
 removed then sliced

2 sprigs laksa leaves (*daun kesom*),
 discard stalks

2 Tbsp water

1. Prepare *rempah*. Place all ingredients in a food processor. Grind into a coarse paste.

2. In a small saucepan, heat oil over medium heat. Add *rempah* and cook until it reaches *pecah minyak* (a process where the oil separates from the paste and turns deep red). Add tamarind water and cook until *rempah* begins to thicken. Season with salt and sugar to taste. Remove from heat.

3. Allow paste to cool before storing in a glass jar.

   *Note:* Mix 1 teaspoon tamarind pulp with 1 tablespoon water to extract 2 teaspoons of tamarind extract

## Cooking with Store-bought Pastes

Flavoursome curries owe their deep complex flavours to the meticulous grinding and blending of fresh aromatics, spices and seasoning. Making *rempah* is such a laborious affair, requiring hours of slicing, dicing, mincing and chopping. These days, the range of ready-made good quality pastes is bewildering. Even garlic and ginger pastes are available. They come in hygienically packed sachets, jars and even cans. Many purists eschew using store-bought pastes but truth be told, they yield reasonably tasty meals.

   For every curry paste, there are numerous brands. The colour, taste and texture of each paste differ, so get to know the basic spices and aromatics that make up authentic curries. Put them to a taste test. Get recommendations from friends or locals.

   Spice pastes are usually concentrated. Always buy a smaller quantity and use it up within one to two cooking sessions. Freeze any excess in a ziplock bag, label it and mark the expiry date. They're generally well-seasoned with salt, so always taste the dish before adding more. For every 500 g (1 lb 1½ oz) meat, 3–3½ tablespoons (45–50 g) of paste is generally sufficient. Add more paste for a more intense curry. If cooking for vegetarians, ensure the paste does not contain meat/seafood ingredients e.g. shrimp paste.

## Thai Green Curry Paste

Makes 170 g (6 oz)

1 tsp coriander seeds (*biji ketumbar*)

½ tsp cumin seeds (*biji jintan putih*)

50 g (1⅔ oz) green bird's eye chillies (*chilli padi hijau*) or 4 large chillies

6 shallots, peeled and roughly chopped

14 cloves Thai garlic*, peeled

Thumb-size galangal (*lengkuas*), peeled and diced

1 kaffir lime, rind only

8 coriander roots, chopped

½ tsp white peppercorns

1 tsp shrimp paste (*belacan*)

1 tsp salt

1. In a small saucepan, dry-fry coriander and cumin seeds over low heat for 5 minutes. Allow to cool before grinding both spices to a powder form in a spice grinder or mortar and pestle.

2. Transfer ground spices to a food processor. Add remaining ingredients except for shrimp paste and salt, and grind into a fairly fine paste.

3. Transfer the paste to a small mixing bowl. Add salt and shrimp paste.

   Note: This is sufficient for 1 recipe. If using normal garlic, 7 cloves suffices. For a less spicy curry, substitute bird's eye chilli with large green chilli or combine bird's eye with large green chilli for a moderately spicy curry.

## Thai Red Curry Paste

This contains similar ingredients as the green curry paste but substitute green chillies with dried red chillies and omit the cumin.

# Meat

Vietnamese Beef Stew Pot Pie 31

Beef Rendang Pie 32

Eurasian Corned Beef Hand Pie 35

Thai Masaman Beef Curry Pot Pie 36

Portuguese Pork and Kidney Bean Shepherd's Pie 39

Pork Vindaloo Curry Pot Pie 40

Pork and Pineapple Pot Pie 43

Nyonya Bak Chang Purses 44

Chinese-style Meat Pie 47

Penang Asam Pork Stew Pot Pie 48

Nyonya Babi Pongteh Shepherd's Pie 51

Giant Mutton Karipap 52

Mutton Rendang Galettes 55

Tip Beef off-cuts comprising trimmings from other cuts of beef and sinew are cheaper and suitable for this stew.

# Vietnamese Beef Stew Pot Pie

Family: Serves 5 • Personal: Makes 5 pies

It's Western and yet Asian at the same time.
This robust meat stew braised with tomato paste and cinnamon,
is given a flavour boost with Asian ingredients like ginger, fish sauce,
lemongrass and a hint of curry powder that makes for a tasty pot pie.

1 egg, lightly beaten for egg wash

**PASTRY**
Plain shortcrust, Puff

**FILLING**
500 g (1 lb 1$^1/_2$ oz) beef brisket,
   diced into 4-cm (1$^1/_2$-in) cubes
2 Tbsp fish sauce
$^1/_2$ tsp meat curry powder
Thumb-size ginger, peeled and
   finely minced
$^1/_2$ tsp ground black pepper +
   more to taste
3 Tbsp oil
2 cloves garlic, peeled and bruised
   with a cleaver
1 stalk lemongrass (*serai*), white
   portion, bruised with a cleaver
5 cm (2 in) cinnamon stick
1 star anise
1 large onion, peeled and diced
2 Tbsp tomato paste
1.5 litres (48 fl oz / 6 cups) water
150 g (5 oz) radish, peeled and
   diced into 2-cm ($^3/_4$-in) cubes
200 g (7 oz) sweet potato, peeled
   and diced into 2-cm ($^3/_4$-in) cubes
2 sprigs Vietnamese mint or laksa
   leaves (*daun kesom*)
$^1/_2$ tsp salt
Ground black pepper, to taste

1. Prepare filling. In a deep mixing bowl, marinate beef with fish sauce, meat curry powder, ginger and ground black pepper for 15 minutes.

2. Heat oil in a medium saucepan over medium heat. Sauté the garlic, lemongrass, cinnamon stick and star anise until aromatic. Toss in onion and sauté until soft.

3. Add marinated beef and continue cooking for another 15 minutes until the meat becomes opaque. Add tomato paste.

4. Add water. Lower heat and let the meat cook for 90 minutes. Add radish and cook for at least 20 minutes, followed by the sweet potato and Vietnamese mint or laksa leaves. Add more water if needed. Continue cooking until beef is tender. Season with salt and ground black pepper to taste.

5. Allow the filling to cool overnight for the flavours to develop before using. Discard lemongrass, star anise, cinnamon stick and mint or laksa leaves.

6. Preheat the oven to 180°C (350°F) for at least 10–15 minutes.

7. **To assemble:** Roll out the dough between 2 pieces of silicon baking sheets or onto a lightly floured surface to a 3 mm ($^1/_8$ in) thickness, with about 3 cm (1$^1/_5$ in) in excess of the pie dish.

8. Spoon filling into each enamel mug to about two-thirds full. Cut the dough 2 cm ($^3/_4$ in) larger than the circumference of the mug to cover the filling. Press the edges below the rim of the mug and seal with a bit of water. Trim excess dough.

9. Create steam holes by making a small cross in the pie top using the tip of a knife. Crimp pie edges as desired. Using a cookie cutter of your choice, cut shapes using pastry trimmings to decorate the pie.

10. Bake for 30–40 minutes or until golden brown.

# Beef Rendang Pie

Family: Serves 4–5 • Personal: Makes 4 pies

Beef brisket is usually marbled with fat and tendon and hence ideal for this pot pie.
The meat is simmered gently in a creamy coconut gravy infused with aromatics such as lemongrass,
turmeric and kaffir lime leaves until fork-tender and semi-dry. A pot pie is a delicious way
to enjoy this signature dish of Malaysian and Indonesian origin.

1 egg, lightly beaten for egg wash

**PASTRY**
Bottom crust– plain shortcrust
Top crust– puff

**REMPAH**
Thumb-size galangal (*lengkuas*),
  peeled and thickly sliced
Thumb-size turmeric (*kunyit*),
  peeled and thickly sliced
6 stalks lemongrass (*serai*),
  white portion, sliced
2 large onions, peeled and diced
8 cloves garlic, peeled and sliced

**FILLING**
500 g (1 lb 1$\frac{1}{2}$ oz) beef brisket,
  cut across the grain into 4-cm
  (1$\frac{1}{2}$-in) cubes
3 tsp salt
3 Tbsp fried chilli paste
  (sambal *tumis*) (page 26*)*
1 tsp ground coriander (*serbuk
  ketumbar*)
50 g (1$\frac{2}{3}$ oz) grated white coconut
  or 3 Tbsp toasted coconut paste
  (*kerisik*)
5 Tbsp oil
2 kaffir lime leaves (*daun limau purut*),
  roughly torn
2 turmeric leaves (*daun kunyit*),
  shredded

1. Prepare *rempah*. Place all ingredients in a food processor and grind into
   a paste.

2. Prepare filling. In a large mixing bowl, season beef with 2 teaspoons of
   salt for 15 minutes.

3. In another mixing bowl, mix *rempah* with sambal *tumis* and ground
   coriander until well-blended. Add to meat and marinate for 30 minutes.

4. Toast grated coconut in a wok or medium saucepan without oil over
   low heat until golden brown. Allow it to cool and then grind into a fine
   consistency using a mortar and pestle (*batu tumbuk*) or a spice grinder.

5. Heat oil in the same wok or saucepan over medium heat. Fry *rempah*
   until aromatic. Add beef and stir-fry until meat is evenly coated with
   the *rempah*.

6. Toss in kaffir lime and turmeric leaves, followed by the tamarind peel
   or tamarind water. Lower heat and add coconut milk. Stew the beef over
   low heat for 90 minutes. Add coconut cream and cook for another
   30 minutes or until the beef is tender.

7. Stir in the toasted grated coconut or *kerisik*. Season with remaining
   salt and sugar. Cook for 10 more minutes until gravy begins to thicken.
   Discard kaffir lime leaves and tamarind peel.

1 piece dried tamarind peel (*asam keping*) or 4 Tbsp tamarind water (To prepare tamarind water, see page 140. Alternatively, use 1–2 tablespoons of store-bought tamarind paste.)

500 ml (8 fl oz / 2 cups) coconut milk (*santan cair*)

375 ml (12 fl oz / 1½ cups) coconut cream (*santan pekat*)

1 Tbsp sugar

*Tip* If using a pressure cooker, it will take 25–30 minutes for the beef to tenderise.

8. Allow the filling to cool down overnight for the flavours to develop before baking.

9. Preheat the oven to 180°C (350°F) for at least 10–15 minutes.

10. **To assemble:** Roll out the dough between 2 pieces of silicon baking sheets or onto a lightly floured surface to a 3 mm (⅛ in) thickness, with about 5 cm (2 in) in excess of the pie dish. Press the bottom pastry firmly onto the base and sides of the pie tray.

11. Spoon filling into the dish until two-thirds full. Cover with puff pastry to conceal the filling. Press top and bottom crusts to seal the edges together. Trim excess dough using a knife and set trimmings aside.

12. Crimp pastry edges with your fingers or use the back of a fork. Brush pie top with egg wash using a pastry brush. Create steam holes by making a small cross in the pie top using the tip of a knife. Using a cookie cutter of your choice, cut shapes using pastry trimmings to decorate the pie.

13. Bake in a perforated pie tray or paper cases with perforated holes for 40–45 minutes or until golden brown.

NOTE: If using store-bought paste, 3½ tablespoons suffices. Add it in step 3.

# Eurasian Corned Beef Hand Pie

Makes 18 hand pies

Moist and succulent, corned beef makes a delectable filling
when spiced with nutmeg. Mixed with vegetables and encased in pastry,
this hand pie is ideal as a snack or finger food for parties.

1 egg, lightly beaten for egg wash

**PASTRY**

Plain shortcrust, Yoghurt
shortcrust, Puff

**FILLING**

4 Tbsp oil

2 large potatoes, peeled and diced
into 0.5-cm ($^1/_4$-in) cubes

1 small carrot, diced into 0.5-cm
($^1/_4$-in) cubes

3 cloves garlic, peeled and roughly
chopped

2 medium onions, peeled and
roughly chopped

60 g ($2^1/_4$ oz) green peas

380 g ($13^1/_2$ oz) canned corned beef,
mashed with a fork

$^1/_2$ tsp ground nutmeg (*serbuk
buah pala*)

$1^1/_2$ tsp salt

1 tsp ground black pepper +
more to taste

1. Prepare filling. Heat oil in a wok or medium saucepan over medium heat.
   Add potatoes and carrot. Stir-fry for 5 minutes. Add garlic and onions.
   Sauté until onions become soft.

2. Toss in the peas, then add corned beef and continue cooking for another
   5 minutes until it is well incorporated with the vegetables. Add nutmeg.
   Season with salt and ground black pepper to taste. Allow the filling to
   cool down before baking.

3. Preheat the oven to 180°F (350°F) for at least 10–15 minutes.

4. **To assemble:** Roll out the dough between 2 pieces of silicon baking
   sheets or onto a lightly floured surface to a 3 mm ($^1/_8$ in) thickness.
   Cut into 15 x 10-cm (6 x 4-in) squares.

5. Spoon 2 tablespoons of filling onto each piece of pastry. Roll the pastry
   over to conceal the filling. Brush water along the pastry edge, press to
   seal the pie. Using a knife, score the top of the hand pie a few times.
   Sprinkle with freshly ground black pepper and press gently into the dough.

6. Brush each pie with egg wash using a pastry brush.

7. Bake for 20–25 minutes or until golden brown.

# Thai Masaman Beef Curry Pot Pie

Family: Serves 4–5 • Personal: Makes 5 pies

This southern Thailand curry is in fact not Thai in its origin. It is said to bear
the influences of Persia, Malaysia and India which employ spices like cardamom,
cloves, cumin and cinnamon, among others. Braised in an aromatic spice paste,
this curry is bold with pronounced spices and is best matched with plain shortcrust pastry.

1 egg, lightly beaten for egg wash

**PASTRY**

Cumin shortcrust, Plain shortcrust, Puff

**SPICE PASTE**

2 cloves

1 Tbsp coriander

1 tsp cumin

$^1/_4$ tsp ground nutmeg

1 tsp black peppercorns

8 dried chillies, seeded and
  soaked in water

1 large onion, peeled and diced

2 stalks lemongrass (serai),
  white portion, sliced

1 whole head of garlic, peeled

Thumb-size galangal (lengkuas), peeled
  and sliced

1 tsp shrimp paste (*belacan*)

2 Tbsp water

**FILLING**

125 ml (4 fl oz / $^1/_2$ cup) coconut cream
  (*santan pekat*)

4 cm (1$^1/_2$ in) cinnamon stick

2 cardamom pods, dry toasted

1 bay leaf

500 g (1 lb 1$^1/_2$ oz) beef brisket or shin,
  cut into 3-cm (1$^1/_5$-in) cubes

2 large onions, peeled and sliced

750 ml (24 fl oz / 3 cups) water

2 tsp chopped Thai palm sugar*

a pinch of salt

1$^1/_2$ tsp tamarind water (*asam jawa*)*
  (see page 140) or 1 tsp lemon juice

3 medium potatoes, peeled and diced
  into 1-cm ($^1/_2$-in) cubes

125 g (4$^1/_2$ oz) roasted peanuts

1. Prepare spice paste. Heat a small saucepan over low heat. Toast cloves, coriander, cumin, nutmeg and peppercorns together until fragrant, then finely grind in a spice grinder. Mix ground spice with remaining ingredients.

2. Prepare filling. Pour coconut cream into a medium saucepan over low heat. Let it come to a simmer, stirring continually until the oil breaks and the cream takes on a glossy sheen.

3. Add spice paste, cinnamon stick, cardamom and bay leaf. Add in the meat and fry until meat turns opaque. Toss in the onion and continue cooking for another 5 minutes.

4. Add water and tamarind water. Let the beef simmer over low heat for 80 minutes. Cook until the meat becomes tender.

5. Add palm sugar, salt and tamarind water or lemon juice. Stir in the potatoes and cook for another 10 minutes. Toss in the roasted peanuts. Discard the bay leaf, cardamom pods and cinnamon stick.

6. Allow the curry to cool overnight for the flavours to develop before baking.

7. Preheat the oven to 180°C (350°F) for at least 10–15 minutes.

8. **To assemble:** Roll out the dough between 2 pieces of silicon baking sheets or onto a lightly floured surface to a 3 mm ($^1/_8$ in) thickness, with about 5 cm (2 in) in excess of the pie dish. Brush edges of the dish with egg wash using a pastry brush.

9. Pour the filling into a deep pie dish. Spoon filling into the dish until two-thirds full. Spread the dough over the filling, pressing down on the edges so that it sticks. Trim excess dough and set trimmings aside.

10. Crimp pastry edges with your fingers or the back of a fork, pressing down all around the rim of the pie dish. Cut trimmings into 3 pieces of 1 x 20-cm ($^1/_2$ x 8-in) long. Braid the dough to line the pie top.

11. Brush pie top with the egg wash. Create steam holes by making a small cross in the pie top using the tip of a knife. Using a cookie cutter of your choice, cut shapes using pastry trimmings to decorate the pie. Bake for 40–45 minutes or until golden brown.

   NOTE: If using store-bought paste, 3$^1/_2$ tablespoons suffices. Add it in step 3.

*Tip* If Thai palm sugar is unavailable, substitute with brown sugar.

*Tip* For a lighter and fluffy potato topping, add 2-3 tablespoons of potato water.

# Portuguese Pork and Kidney Bean Shepherd's Pie

Family: Makes 3 pies, each serving 10–12 • Personal: Makes 10 pies

This shepherd's pie is an Asian take on the Brazilian *feijoada* (meat and black bean stew) where Chinese sausage is added to this tasty Portuguese stew. Cooked with vegetables, this well-balanced pie with a potato topping is absolutely delicious when simmered with naturally sweet tasting meat like pork.

600 g (1 lb 5$^1$/$_3$ oz) (6 large potatoes) peeled, boiled and mashed with 2 tsp salt

1 egg, lightly beaten for egg wash

**PASTRY**
Potatoes, Plain shortcrust, Puff

**FILLING**
6 Tbsp oil + more if needed

2 Chinese sausages (*lapcheong*), thickly sliced

2 cloves garlic, peeled and roughly chopped

2 medium onions, peeled and diced

500 g (1 lb 1$^1$/$_2$ oz) pork belly, cut into 3-cm (1$^1$/$_5$-in) cubes

1 small carrot, diced into 2-cm ($^3$/$_4$-in) cubes

1 small radish, diced into 2-cm ($^3$/$_4$-in) cubes

6 cabbage leaves, thickly sliced

125 ml (4 fl oz / $^1$/$_2$ cup) chicken stock

250 ml (8 fl oz / 1 cup) water

425 g (15 oz) canned kidney beans, drained

425 g (15 oz) canned chick peas, drained

Salt to taste

Ground white pepper to taste

1. Prepare filling. Heat 2 tablespoons of oil in a wok or medium saucepan over low heat. Add Chinese sausages and stir fry for 1 minute until fragrant. Remove from heat and set aside.

2. Add remaining 4 tablespoons of oil, toss in the garlic and onions. Sauté onions until soft.

3. Add pork belly and cook for 10 minutes until the meat turns opaque. Mix in the carrot and radish. Simmer for 25 minutes over low heat.

4. Add cabbage, chicken stock and water. Cook until cabbage has softened. Add kidney beans and chick peas and cook for another 10 minutes. Return Chinese sausages to wok or saucepan. Season with salt and pepper. Allow the filling to cool down overnight for the flavours to develop before baking.

5. Preheat the oven to 180°C (350°F) for at least 10–15 minutes.

6. **To assemble:** Using a slotted spoon, spoon stew into the dish to two thirds full. Spread the mashed potato over the filling. Brush potato with egg wash using a pastry brush. Using a fork, score lines on the mashed potatoes.

7. Bake for 40–45 minutes or until golden brown.

# Pork Vindaloo Curry Pot Pie

Family: Serves 5 • Personal: Makes 4 pies

Perky and tangy from the use of vinegar and garlic, this much-loved Indian
curry has its origins in Portugal. When vindaloo was transported to Goa, a coastal state
in western India by Portuguese pioneers, it adapted a spicy kick made peppery from the
addition of peppercorns, mustard and other spices. My first taste of this rich vindaloo curry
was in Japan when I cooked it for a group of Singaporeans, thanks to a home-made
curry paste concocted by Uncle James, Angie's father.

1 egg, lightly beaten for egg wash

**PASTRY**
Puff, Plain shortcrust

**SPICE PASTE**
1 tsp cumin seeds (*jintan putih*)

2 tsp mustard seeds (*biji sawi*)

1 tsp white peppercorns

6 dried whole chillies, seeded and
soaked in 5 Tbsp vinegar

6 cloves garlic, peeled

Thumb-size ginger, peeled and
roughly chopped

Half thumb-size turmeric, peeled
and roughly chopped

3 large onions, peeled and diced

2 tsp garam masala

**FILLING**
2 Tbsp ghee

3 cm (1$^1$/$_2$ in) cinnamon stick

2 cardamom pods

500 g (1 lb 1$^1$/$_2$ oz) pork belly,
diced into 4-cm (1$^1$/$_2$-in) cubes

625 ml (20 fl oz / 2$^1$/$_2$ cups) water

2 large green chillies, seeded and
diagonally sliced

Salt to taste

1 tsp jaggery* (Indian palm sugar)

1. Prepare spice paste. Heat a wok or medium saucepan over medium heat. Dry fry cumin and mustard seeds and peppercorns until fragrant. Allow to cool down and then grind into a powder in a spice grinder or a mortar and pestle. Meanwhile, place remaining ingredients in a food processor and grind into a paste. Mix together with the ground spices in a small mixing bowl until incorporated. Set aside.

2. Prepare filling. Add ghee into the same saucepan, then add cinnamon stick and cardamoms and fry for 2 minutes. Return spice paste to heat and cook until aromatic.

3. Add pork belly and cook until meat turns opaque. Add water and green chillies and let the curry simmer for 30 minutes until pork is tender. Season with salt and jaggery to taste. Allow filling to cool overnight for the flavours to develop before baking. Discard cardamom and cinnamon stick.

4. Preheat the oven to 180°C (350°F) for at least 10–15 minutes.

5. Spoon filling into the dish to about two-thirds full.

6. **To assemble:** Roll out the dough between 2 pieces of silicon baking sheets or onto a lightly floured surface to a 3 mm ($^1$/$_8$ in) thickness, with about 5 cm (2 in) in excess of the pie dish or case.

7. Cover the filling with the dough. Press against the sides of the pie dish to seal the pastry. Trim excess using a knife. Crimp as desired.

8. Using a cookie cutter of your choice, cut shapes using pastry trimmings to decorate the pie.

9. Brush pie top with egg wash using a pastry brush. Create steam holes by making a small cross in the pie top using the tip of a knife.

10. Bake for 50–60 minutes or until golden brown.

NOTE: If using store-bought paste, 3$^1$/$_2$ tablespoons suffices. Add it in step 2.

*Tip* If jaggery is unavailable, substitute with brown sugar.

Tip For a more pungent curry, add one cinnamon stick and 2 star anises during step 3.

# Pork and Pineapple Pot Pie

Family: Serves 7–8 • Personal: Makes 7 pies

The tropical flavours of this curry pie burst forth on the palate with
the fruity accents of pineapple. The burnt-orange oil from the *rempah* gives
the appearance that it's spicy but it is in fact mild on the 'spice-o-meter'.
Although pineapple is naturally sweet, Sarah's tip is to add a pinch of
sugar to accentuate the sweetness of the gravy.

1 egg, lightly beaten for egg wash

cloves, as needed

### PASTRY
Atta shortcrust, Plain shortcrust,
   Yoghurt shortcrust, Puff

### REMPAH
2 cloves garlic, peeled

Thumb-size fresh ginger, peeled
   and sliced

Thumb-size galangal (*lengkuas*),
   peeled and sliced

6 dried chillies, soaked in hot water
   until soft and seeded

4 fresh chillies, seeded

Thumb-size fresh turmeric (*kunyit*),
   peeled and sliced

### FILLING
100 ml oil (3$^{1}/_{2}$ fl oz / $^{1}/_{2}$ cup)

2 stalks lemongrass (*serai*),
   white portion only, bruised

10 shallots, peeled and roughly
   chopped

750 g (1$^{1}/_{2}$ lb) pork belly, cut into
   3-cm (1$^{1}/_{5}$-in) cubes

5 tsp meat curry powder

500 ml (16 fl oz / 2 cups) water

Salt to taste

Sugar to taste

$^{1}/_{2}$ pineapple, peeled, cored and
   'eyes' removed

1. Prepare *rempah*. Place all ingredients in a food processor and grind
   into a paste.

2. Prepare filling. Heat oil in a wok or medium saucepan over medium heat.
   Add lemongrass, shallots and *rempah*. Fry until fragrant.

3. Add pork belly and continue cooking for 1 minute. Add meat curry powder
   and fry until the meat turns opaque.

4. Add water and bring to a boil over high heat. Lower heat, then simmer
   until the meat is tender and the gravy becomes thick. Season with salt
   and sugar to taste.

5. Toss in the pineapple and let it simmer for another 5 minutes. Allow filling
   to cool down overnight for the flavours to develop before baking.

6. Preheat oven to 180°C (350°F) for at least 10–15 minutes.

7. **To assemble:** Roll out the dough between 2 pieces of silicon baking sheet
   or onto a lightly floured surface to a 3 mm ($^{1}/_{8}$ in) thickness, with about
   5 cm (2 in) in excess to cover the top of the pie bowl. Trim excess dough,
   then crimp pastry edges with your fingers.

8. Decorate pie top with whole cloves and pastry trimmings as desired.

9. Brush pie top with the egg wash using a pastry brush. Create steam holes
   by making a small cross in the pie top using the tip of a knife.

10. Bake for 30 minutes or until golden brown. Allow pie to stand for
    10 minutes before cutting.

# Nyonya Bak Chang Purses

*Makes 12 bak chang*

Each time we bite into a *bak chang* (rice dumpling stuffed with meat),
it evokes childhood memories of home-made *chang* boiling in oil tins over charcoal stoves.
Labour-intensive, it requires many helping hands to individually wrap each dumpling with
bamboo and pandan leaves before boiling them for 5–6 hours. We refreshed Aunt Tan Kiah Whee's
recipe by encasing the flavourful meat-filled *chang* in crisp buttery phyllo pastry
that turns the flavour dial one notch up. So *shiok*!

100 g (3¹/₂ oz) steamed glutinous rice, soaked in water for 4 hours

1 Tbsp oil

15 blue pea flowers, soaked in 60 ml (2 fl oz / ¹/₄ cup) hot water

**PASTRY**

Phyllo

**FILLING**

1 Tbsp oil

20 cloves garlic, peeled and minced

8 shallots, peeled and diced finely

40 g (1¹/₄ oz) sand ginger (*cekur*), peeled and diced finely

600 g (1 lb 5¹/₃ oz) pork belly, parboil for 5 minutes and cut into 2-cm (³/₄-in) cubes

5 dried Chinese mushrooms, soaked and diced into 1-cm (¹/₂-in) cubes

150 g (5 oz) candied winter melon (*dong gua*), diced into 1-cm (¹/₂-in) cubes

250 ml (8 fl oz / 1 cup) water

80 g (2⁴/₅ oz) ground coriander (*serbuk ketumbar*)

1 Tbsp dark soy sauce

1 tsp salt

1 Tbsp ground white pepper

1. Prepare filling. Heat oil in a work or medium saucepan over medium heat. Sauté garlic, shallots and sand ginger until soft and aromatic. Add pork belly and continue to cook until meat turns opaque.

2. Toss in the Chinese mushrooms and winter melon. Continue cooking, adding some water if the meat mixture is too dry. Add ground coriander and dark soy sauce. Season with salt and pepper to taste.

3. Allow filling to cool down overnight for the flavours to develop before baking.

4. Wash the glutinous rice and transfer to a 20 cm (8 in) round tray lined with a muslin cloth. Steam rice over high heat for 15–20 minutes until cooked. Remove the tray immediately from heat. Sprinkle a few drops of blue pea flower water randomly over the rice. Leave to cool.

5. Preheat oven to 180°C (350°F) for at least 10–15 minutes.

6. **To assemble:** Roll out 2 sheets of phyllo pastry. Cut into 20-cm (8-in) squares. Using a pastry brush, brush each square piece with oil. For each parcel, stack 2 pastry squares on top of each other.

7. Spread 2 tablespoons of steamed rice onto the phyllo pastry. Spoon 1 tablespoon filling over the rice. Cover with another layer of steamed rice and drizzle more blue water on it. Fold the phyllo over to enclose the filling to resemble a 'purse'.

8. Place them onto a baking sheet that has been lightly oiled. Bake for 40 minutes or until golden brown.

# Chinese-style Meat Pie

Makes 12 pies

Sarah's family loves Chinese-style meat pies (*siew pau*).
Her late mother would often bake a batch with ingredients of their choice.
Unlike Chinese pastry which is layered and flaky,
Sarah developed a delicious shortcrust pastry with yoghurt that is pliable,
resilient and yet tender. It pairs deliciously with the filling.

1 egg, lightly beaten with 1 Tbsp oil, for egg wash

2 Tbsp white sesame seeds

**PASTRY**

Plain shortcrust, Yoghurt shortcrust, Puff

**FILLING**

80 g (2⅘ oz) prawns, shelled and cut into 1-cm (½-in) cubes

100 g (3½ oz) pork, cut into 1-cm (½-in) cubes

2 Tbsp green peas

60 g (2¼ oz) barbecued roast pork (*char siew*), cut into 1-cm (½-in) cubes

3 Chinese dried mushrooms, soaked in hot water and diced into 1-cm (½-in) cubes

2 tsp light soy sauce

½ Tbsp dark soy sauce

A pinch of ground white pepper

1 Tbsp cornflour

1 slice ham, cut into 1-cm (½-in) cubes

1 egg, lightly beaten

1 tsp sesame oil

1 tsp salt

2 tsp sugar

2 Tbsp oil

1 medium onion, peeled and diced

1. Prepare filling. In a large mixing bowl, mix prawns, pork, green peas, barbecued roast pork, Chinese mushrooms, light soy sauce, dark soy sauce, pepper, cornflour and ham together with the egg. Mix well. Add sesame oil, salt and sugar. Mix until well incorporated.

2. Heat oil in a wok or medium saucepan over medium heat. Sauté the onion until aromatic. Add to the meat mixture to marinate for 1 hour and chill until ready to bake.

3. Preheat oven to 180°C (350°F) for at least 10–15 minutes.

4. **To assemble:** Roll out the dough between 2 pieces of silicon baking sheets or onto a lightly floured surface to a 3 mm (⅛ in) thickness. Using a round cutter, cut the pastry large enough to fit into a muffin cup.

5. Spoon a teaspoon of filling over the pastry. Crimp the edges to make wavy edges.

6. Brush pastry edges with egg wash using a pastry brush. Sprinkle white sesame seeds over the filling.

7. Bake for 40–45 minutes or until golden brown.

8. Allow pies to cool for 10 minutes. Use a palette knife and gently ease pies out of each muffin cup.

# Penang Asam Pork Stew Pot Pie

Family: Serves 4 • Personal: Makes 4 pies

While a Chinese stew is one where the meat is usually braised in soy,
garlic and Chinese Shaoxing rice wine, this one has been tempered with
the acidity of tamarind and toasty shrimp paste. The flavourful concoction
pairs so well with plain shortcrust pastry.

1 egg, lightly beaten for egg wash

**PASTRY**
Atta shortcrust, Plain shortcrust, Puff

**FILLING**
$^1/_2$ Tbsp toasted shrimp paste (*belacan*)

1 Tbsp oil

2 cloves garlic, peeled and roughly chopped

1 large onion, peeled and diced

1 Tbsp sugar

400 g ($14^1/_3$ oz) pork belly, cut into 4-cm ($1^1/_2$-in) pieces

250 ml (8 fl oz / 1 cup) water

1 piece of tamarind peel (*asam keping*) or 4 Tbsp tamarind water*

2 tsp Chinese Shaoxing wine

1 Tbsp dark soy sauce

Salt to taste

1. Prepare filling. Heat a wok or medium saucepan over medium heat. Add shrimp paste and toast for 1 minute. Using the spatula, break up the shrimp paste. Add oil and sauté garlic and onion until soft.

2. Sprinkle sugar over the garlic-onion mixture and cook until the sugar caramelises. Add pork belly and continue cooking until meat turns opaque. Add water and toss in the tamarind peel or tamarind water.

3. Reduce to low heat and let the meat simmer for 20–25 minutes or until tender. Add the Shaoxing wine and dark soy sauce. Season with salt to taste. Cook for another 5 minutes, then turn the heat off.

4. Allow filling to cool overnight for the flavours to develop before baking. Discard the tamarind peel.

5. Preheat oven to 180°C (350°F) for at least 10–15 minutes.

6. **To assemble:** Roll out the dough between 2 pieces of silicon baking sheets or onto a lightly floured surface to a 3 mm ($^1/_8$ in) thickness, with about 5 cm (2 in) in excess of the 250 ml (8 fl oz / 1 cup) Chinese rice bowls.

7. Spoon filling into each bowl to about two-thirds full. Using your finger dipped in water, run it along on the edge of the bowl. Cover filling with the dough. Trim excess using a knife and set trimmings aside. Crimp as desired.

8. Using a cookie cutter of your choice, cut shapes using pastry trimmings to decorate the pie. Brush pies tops with egg wash using a pastry brush. Create steam holes by making a small cross in the pie top using the tip of a knife.

9. Bake for 40–45 minutes or until golden brown.

*NOTE: To prepare tamarind water, see page 140. Alternatively, use 1–2 tablespoons of store-bought tamarind paste.

# Nyonya Babi Pongteh Shepherd's Pie

Family: Serves 8–9 • Personal: Makes 8 pies

For this Peranakan classic, Sarah's version has two types of preserved salted
soy beans: salty and sweet fermented bean paste. They yield a sweeter
and a more full-bodied mouthful of soy beans on the palate.
The morsels of meat, coaxed to tenderness after gentle braising, is absolutely *shiok*
as a shepherd's pie. Alternatively, puff pastry is just as delicious.

1 Chinese coriander (cilantro),
   finely chopped

**PASTRY**
Atta shortcrust, Plain shortcrust, Puff

**TOPPING**
450 g (1 lb) (4–5 potatoes), peeled,
   boiled and mashed

**FILLING**
6 Tbsp oil

100 g (3¹/₂ oz) shallots, peeled and
   finely sliced

1 whole head of garlic, peeled and
   minced

600 g (1 lb 5¹/₃ oz) pork belly,
   cut into 1-cm (¹/₂-in) cubes

10 Chinese dried mushrooms, soaked
   until softened and diced into 1-cm
   (¹/₂-in) cubes

1¹/₂ Tbsp fermented salted bean paste
   (salted *taucheo*)

1 Tbsp fermented sweet bean paste
   (sweet *taucheo*)*

1 fresh red chilli, diced into 1-cm
   (¹/₂-in) cubes

2 Tbsp brown sugar

750 ml (24 fl oz / 3 cups) water

¹/₂ Tbsp dark soy sauce

¹/₄ tsp salt

1. Prepare filling. Heat oil in a wok or medium saucepan over medium heat. Sauté the shallots and garlic until soft and aromatic.

2. Add pork belly and fry until meat turns opaque. Add Chinese mushrooms, salted bean paste and sweet bean paste, chilli and brown sugar. Stir until well incorporated.

3. Add water and allow the meat to simmer over low heat for 30 minutes or until pork is tender. Add dark soy sauce and season with salt.

4. Allow the filling to cool down overnight for the flavours to develop before baking.

5. Preheat oven to 180°C (350°F) for at least 10–15 minutes.

6. **To assemble:** Scoop filling into a deep dish until two-thirds full.

7. Fill a piping bag with mashed potatoes and pipe it over the filling. Bake for 30 minutes until potato topping is golden brown.

8. Serve pie piping hot. For each serving, sprinkle with finely chopped coriander.

   *NOTE: Omit if unavailable.

# Giant Mutton Karipap

Makes seven 20-cm (8-in) *karipaps*

For this *karipap*, Sarah developed a delicious pastry with yoghurt
to complement the mutton filling that's infused with the earthy aromas of cumin,
fennel and the peppery punch of white peppercorns. She loves mutton and would
opt for *karipap kambing* (mutton curry puffs) over *goreng pisang* (banana fritters)
and *epok epok* (potato curry puffs) anytime.

1 egg, lightly beaten for egg wash

**PASTRY**

Atta shortcrust, Plain shortcrust,
  Yoghurt shortcrust, Puff

**FILLING**

4 Tbsp oil

4 medium potatoes, peeled and diced
  into 1-cm (¹/₂-in) cubes

1 large onion, peeled and diced

4 cloves garlic, peeled and thinly sliced

4 medium shallots, peeled and
  thinly sliced

1 Tbsp ground cumin (*serbuk jintan
  putih*)

1 Tbsp ground fennel (*serbuk jintan
  manis*)

500 g (1 lb 1¹/₂ oz) mutton, cut into
  1-cm (¹/₂-in) cubes

3–4 Tbsp water

Salt to taste

1 tsp ground white pepper

1 parsley, cut into 2-cm (³/₄-in) lengths

1 spring onion (scallion), cut into 2-cm
  (³/₄-in) lengths

1. Prepare filling. Heat oil in a wok or medium saucepan over medium heat.
   Fry the potatoes for 2 minutes, followed by onion, garlic and shallots.
   Add ground cumin and fennel and sauté until aromatic.

2. Add mutton and continue to cook until the meat turns opaque, adding
   a little water if it is too dry. Season with salt and pepper to taste. Toss
   in the parsley and spring onion.

3. Allow filling to cool down overnight, for the flavours to develop
   before baking.

4. Preheat oven to 180°C (350°F) for at least 10–15 minutes.

5. **To assemble:** Roll out the dough between 2 pieces of silicon baking sheets
   or onto a lightly floured surface to a 3 mm (¹/₈ in) thickness.

6. Using a 20 cm (8 in) round cutter, cut out dough circles. Scoop filling on
   one side of dough. Brush pastry edges with water then fold the other half
   over the filling. Press the edges together using your fingers to seal. Crimp
   using finger and thumb. Brush pie top with egg wash using a pastry brush.

7. Bake for 40–50 minutes or until golden brown.

# Mutton Rendang Galettes

Makes 12 galettes

A galette is a French word for rustic free-form tarts with hand-folded edges.
Mutton has assertive gamey flavours. There are many versions of the mutton *rendang*
and this one among Sarah's favourite was developed by her friend,
Mahes who uses yoghurt instead of tomato to give it more
acidity for more rounded and well balanced flavours.

1 egg, lightly beaten for egg wash

**PASTRY**
Flaky, Atta shortcrust,
   Plain shortcrust

**SPICE PASTE**
$^1/_2$ tsp fennel (*jintan manis*)
$^1/_2$ tsp cumin (*jintan putih*)
1 tsp coriander (*ketumbar*)

**FILLING**
1.25 litres (40 fl oz / 5 cups) water
   + more if needed
500 g (1 lb 1$^1/_2$ oz) mutton meat,
   diced into 4-cm (1$^1/_2$-in) cubes
Thumb-size ginger, peeled
   and minced
2 cloves garlic, peeled and minced
1 potato, peeled and cut into quarters
1 Tbsp meat curry powder
1 Tbsp chilli powder
Salt to taste
2 Tbsp oil
2 cm ($^3/_4$ in) cinnamon stick
3 star anise
2 cardamoms, lightly crushed
10 medium shallots, peeled and
   finely sliced
2 sprigs curry leaves, discard stalks
1 Tbsp yoghurt
3 sprigs Chinese coriander (cilantro)

1. Prepare spice paste. Place all ingredients in a spice grinder or mortar and pestle and grind into a powder.

2. Prepare filling. Bring 500 ml (16 fl oz / 2 cups) water to a boil in a medium saucepan over high heat. Toss in mutton to scald it. This strips the meat of some oil. Drain the mutton and return it into the saucepan.

3. Add ginger, garlic and remaining 750 ml (24 fl oz / 3 cups) water, making sure it covers the meat. Bring to a boil, then reduce the heat to low. Simmer for 10 minutes, then add in the potato. When water is reduced by half, mix in the meat curry powder, chilli powder and spice paste. Season with salt to taste. Continue to simmer until meat is tender.

4. In another saucepan, add oil and fry the cinnamon, star anise, cardamom and shallots until fragrant. Toss in the curry leaves and mix it into the mutton. Season with salt to taste. If the curry is too dry, add 2–4 tablespoons of water. Mix in yoghurt and coriander leaves until incorporated. Allow the filling to cool down overnight for the flavours to develop before using.

5. Preheat oven to 180°C (350°F) for at least 10–15 minutes.

6. **To assemble:** Roll out the dough between 2 pieces of silicon baking sheets or onto a lightly floured surface to a 3 mm ($^1/_8$ in) thickness.

7. Cut pastry into 15 x 14-cm (6 x 5$^1/_2$ in) pieces. Spoon 1 tablespoon of filling into the centre, then fold 3 cm (1$^1/_2$ in) inwards along all the edges. Press dough down gently until it sticks.

8. Brush dough with egg wash using a pastry brush. Bake for 40–50 minutes or until golden brown.

# Poultry

Sarah's Classic Chicken Pie 59

Chicken Sausage Pie 60

Green Chicken Rendang Pot Pie 63

Thai Green Chicken Curry Pot Pie 64

Ayam Korma Shepherd's Pie 67

Ayam Masak Merah Pot Pie 68

Indonesian Opor Ayam Pot Pie 71

Satay Chicken Pie 72

Butter Chicken Pot Pie 75

Beggar's Chicken 76

Nyonya Ayam Buah Keluak Pot Pie 79

Thai Roast Duck Red Curry Pot Pie 80

Masala Turkey and Cranberry Chutney Pie 82

# Sarah's Classic Chicken Pie

Family: Serves 6–7 • Personal: Makes 6 pies

Sarah ate her first chicken pie at a defunct café when she was just 7 years old.
Four years later, Sarah savoured home-made chicken pie at a birthday party. She was hooked
to the pastry and decided to bake her own pie. Her first attempts at baking
chicken pies weren't successful so she baked it again and again and yet again.
After countless chow-downs, her chicken pie became much-loved!

1 egg, lightly beaten for egg wash

**PASTRY**
Atta shortcrust, Plain shortcrust, Puff

**FILLING**
75 ml ($2^2/_5$ fl oz / $^3/_4$ cup) oil

1 large onion, peeled and coarsely
chopped

400 g ($14^1/_3$ oz) chicken, cut into
3-cm ($1^1/_5$-in) cubes

1 carrot, peeled and diced into
2-cm ($^3/_4$-in) cubes

375 ml (12 fl oz / $1^1/_2$ cups) water

65 g ($2^1/_4$ oz) canned button
mushrooms, sliced

1 chicken stock cube

Salt to taste

Ground white pepper to taste

Roux: 2 Tbsp plain (all-purpose) flour,
mixed with 1 Tbsp water to form
a paste

60 g ($2^1/_4$ oz) green peas

1. Prepare filling. Heat oil in a wok or medium saucepan over medium heat.
   Sauté onion until aromatic.

2. Add chicken, followed by the carrot and stir-fry for 5 minutes. Add water
   and simmer until water is reduced to half.

3. Add mushrooms and chicken stock cube. Season with salt and pepper.
   Continue cooking until chicken is tender.

4. Add roux to thicken the gravy, stirring continually to prevent it from
   sticking to the bottom of the pot. Toss in the green peas and stir into
   the mixture.

5. Allow the filling to cool down overnight for the flavours to develop
   before baking.

6. Preheat oven to 180°C (350°F) for at least 10–15 minutes.

7. **To assemble:** Roll out the dough between 2 pieces of silicon baking
   sheet or onto a lightly floured surface to a 3 mm ($^1/_8$ in) thickness large
   enough to fit into the base of the pie dish.

8. Press dough firmly down to the base and side of the dish. Trim off
   excess dough and set it aside. Spoon filling over the pastry. Using the
   same method, roll out the remaining dough. To make heart cut-outs to
   form the top crust, use heart-shaped cutters, overlapping it over the top
   of the filling.

9. Brush pie top with the egg wash using a pastry brush. Bake for
   40–50 minutes or until golden brown.

# Chicken Sausage Pie

Makes 5 braided pies

Turkey used to be very expensive in a small town like Kluang, Johor
in Malaysia during Sarah's childhood days. The filling is actually
the stuffing meant for roast turkey traditionally served during Christmas.
Sarah substituted English chestnuts with Chinese water chestnuts for a
sweet, juicy and crunchy bite. She braided the pastry to enhance its visual appeal.

1 egg, lightly beaten for egg wash

**PASTRY**
Puff

**FILLING**
340 g (12¼ oz) chicken frankfurters, remove the casings

2 slices ham, cut into 1-cm (½-in) pieces

425 g (15 oz) canned button mushrooms, coarsely chopped

6 water chestnuts, peeled and roughly chopped

3 Tbsp oil

1 large onion, peeled and finely chopped

1 clove garlic, peeled and finely minced

1 egg

1 bunch Chinese coriander (cilantro), finely chopped

1 tsp ground black pepper

5 Tbsp breadcrumbs

1 chicken stock cube

A dash of Worcestershire sauce

1 Tbsp brandy (optional)

Salt to taste

1. Prepare filling. Using a fork, mash chicken frankfurters in a large mixing bowl. Mix in the ham, button mushrooms and water chestnuts.

2. Heat oil in a wok or medium saucepan over medium heat. Sauté the onion and garlic until soft and aromatic. Add into the meat mixture.

3. Lastly, break in an egg. Add the Chinese coriander, black pepper, breadcrumbs, chicken stock cube, Worcestershire sauce and brandy, if using. Season with salt to taste. Prepare the filling a day earlier and chill overnight.

4. Preheat oven to 180°C (350°F) for at least 10–15 minutes.

5. **To assemble:** Prepare a 24 cm (9.5 in) square puff pastry and spoon the filling into the centre of the pastry dough.

6. With a butter knife, cut both sides of the pastry 2-cm (¾-in) diagonally apart to make strips. Pleat it across each side, first to the right, then to the left, overlapping each other to enclose the filling. Brush pie top with egg wash using a pastry brush.

7. Bake for 40–45 minutes or until golden brown.

*Tip* Chicken sausage meat can be substituted with pork or beef.

   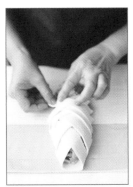 

*Tip* Removing the chicken skin is healthier and results in a less oily curry.

# Green Chicken Rendang Pot Pie

Family: Serves 4–5 • Personal: Makes 5 pies

*Rendang*, a signature curry of Indonesia and Malaysia is simmered
with spices and aromatics until dry yet still moist. I tasted this
fragrant Johor chicken rendang cooked by Makcik Zaleha in Malacca, Malaysia.
After some persuasion, the affable *makcik* (aunt in Malay) revealed that finely
shredded kaffir lime and turmeric leaves were added to boost its aromatic flavours.

oil or melted butter, as needed

**PASTRY**

Plain shortcrust, Phyllo, Puff

**REMPAH**

2 cloves garlic, peeled and roughly chopped

6 shallots, peeled and diced

10 green chillies, seeded, cut into 2-cm (³/₄-in) pieces

Thumb-size ginger, peeled and diced

Thumb-size galangal *(lengkuas)*, peeled and sliced

Thumb-size turmeric *(kunyit)*, peeled and sliced

3 stalks lemongrass *(serai)*, white portion, sliced

2 candlenuts *(buah keras)*, crushed

**FILLING**

3 Tbsp oil

2 sprigs kaffir lime leaves *(daun limau purut)*

1 small turmeric leaf *(daun kunyit)*, knotted

Water, as needed

500 g (1 lb 1¹/₂ oz) free-range *(kampung)* chicken meat, cut into 3-cm (1¹/₅-in) cubes

60 ml (2 fl oz / ¹/₄ cup) coconut milk *(santan cair)*

60 ml (2 fl oz / ¹/₄ cup) coconut cream *(santan pekat)*

¹/₂ tsp salt

1 Tbsp sugar

1 piece tamarind peel *(asam keping)* or tamarind water

1. Prepare *rempah*. Place all ingredients in a food processor and grind into a paste. If using a mortar and pestle, start pounding the hard ingredients followed by the rest of the ingredients.

2. Prepare filling. Heat oil in a wok or medium saucepan over medium heat. Add *rempah*, kaffir lime leaves and turmeric leaf. Sauté until the *rempah* becomes aromatic, adding 1–2 tablespoons water if required.

3. Add chicken and cook until the meat turns opaque. Add coconut milk and simmer for 20 minutes over low heat until meat is tender. Add coconut cream and continue cooking until the gravy thickens. Season with salt and sugar to taste. Add tamarind peel or tamarind water.

4. Allow the filling to cool down overnight for the flavours to develop before baking.

5. Preheat oven to 180°C (350°F) for at least 10–15 minutes.

6. **To assemble:** Using a slotted spoon, spoon curry into the dish to two-thirds full. Brush three sheets of phyllo with oil or melted butter. Trim excess pastry and set it aside. For the remaining sheets, cut into 10-cm (4-in) squares. Brush each piece of phyllo sheet with oil or melted butter. Stack 2 pastry squares on top of one another. Scrunch each stack with your fingers and place it on top on the filling. Repeat until the filling is covered with pastry.

7. Bake for 40–45 minutes or until golden brown. Serve piping hot.

   NOTE: To prepare tamarind water, see page 140. Alternatively, use 1–2 tablespoons of store-bought tamarind paste.

# Thai Green Chicken Curry Pot Pie

Family: Serves 6–7 • Personal: Makes 7 pies

Pierce through the flaky puff pastry and let the heady aromas of
this Thai green chicken curry waft in the air. This authentic curry made with
green chilli is an adaption of Thai hotel chef Hannarin Rawpang's recipe.
His version is flavourful with citrusy and lemony nuances from the kaffir lime leaves
and *krachai* (razor galangal). It is further accented by aniseed flavours from Thai basil.

1 egg, lightly beaten for egg wash

**PASTRY**
Plain shortcrust, Phyllo, Puff

**FILLING**
125 ml (4 fl oz / ¹/₂ cup) coconut cream
  (*santan pekat*)

450 g (14 oz) chicken meat, cut into
  cubes

Thumb-size razor galangal (krachai),
  peeled and bruised

1 stalk lemongrass (serai), white
  portion, bruised

4 Tbsp green curry paste (page 27,
  alternatively use store-bought paste)

1 litre (32 fl oz/ 4 cups) water

250 g (9 oz) round green aubergines
  (eggplants), cut into 2-cm (³/₄-in)
  cubes

100 g (3¹/₂ oz) pea aubergines
  (eggplants)

1 tsp Thai palm sugar*, grated

2 kaffir lime leaves (*daun limau purut*)

salt to taste

1 tsp fish sauce

a handful of Thai basil leaves

*Tip* If Thai palm sugar is
unavailable, substitute with
brown sugar. Substitute razor
galangal with sand ginger.

1. Prepare filling. In a saucepan, add coconut cream and bring to a simmer over low heat. Cook until the oil from the coconut milk breaks (this is a process where a thin film of oil forms), then add in chicken, razor galangal, lemongrass and green curry paste. Simmer for about 10 minutes until the meat is tender or until the sauce begins to thicken.

2. In a separate saucepan, fill with water and bring to a boil over low heat. Once boiled, add both green and pea aubergines. Allow aubergines to cook for 10 minutes until they start to soften.

3. Add Thai palm sugar, followed by the kaffir lime leaves. Continue to cook for 1 more minute, then season with salt and fish sauce before turning the heat off. Toss in the Thai basil leaves.

4. Allow filling to cool down overnight for flavours to develop before baking. Discard lemongrass, razor galangal and kaffir lime leaves.

5. Preheat the oven to 180°C (350°F) for at least 10–15 minutes.

6. **To assemble:** Roll out the dough between 2 pieces of silicon baking sheets or onto a lightly floured surface to a 3 mm (¹/₈ in) thickness, with about 5 cm (2 in) in excess of the 12.5 x 7.5 cm (5 x 3 in) pie dish or cases.

7. Cover the filling with the dough. Crimp pie edges as desired. Using trimmings, cut 1 x 20-cm (¹/₂ x 8-in) to decorate pie top. Create steam holes by making a few crosses in the pie top using the tip of a knife. Brush pie top with egg wash using a pastry brush.

8. Bake for 40 minutes or until golden brown. Serve piping hot.

   NOTE: If using store-bought Thai green curry paste, 3¹/₂ tablespoons suffices. Add it in step 1.

# Ayam Korma Shepherd's Pie

Family: Serve 5 • Personal: Makes 5 pies

Sarah's friend who cooks very good Indian curries makes a scrumptious Ayam Korma
that is lip-smackingly tasty. What makes her version appetising is ground cashew nuts
that not only thickens the korma but renders it creamy and nutty!

4 large potatoes, peeled and boiled for
10 minutes then sliced into 3-mm
($^{1}/_{8}$-in) thick pieces

1 egg, lightly beaten for egg wash

fried curry leaves, for garnish

## PASTRY
Atta shortcrust, Plain shortcrust, Puff

## REMPAH
1 green chilli, seeded

40 g ($1^{1}/_{4}$ oz) cashew nuts

125 g (4 oz) freshly grated skinned
coconut

## FILLING
125 ml (4 fl oz / $^{1}/_{2}$ cup) oil

2 cardamoms (*buah pelaga*), bruised

1 star anise (*bunga lawang*)

4 cm ($1^{1}/_{2}$ in) cinnamon stick (*kayu manis*)

2 stalks curry leaves, discard stalks

1 large onion, peeled and sliced

1 Tbsp ginger paste

$^{1}/_{2}$ tsp garlic paste

500 g ($1^{1}/_{2}$ oz) chicken, diced into
3-cm ($1^{1}/_{5}$-in) cubes

60 ml (2 fl oz / $^{1}/_{2}$ cup) water

1 medium carrot, peeled and diced

1 Tbsp ground coriander (*serbuk ketumbar*)

$^{1}/_{2}$ Tbsp ground fennel (*serbuk
jintan manis*)

$^{1}/_{2}$ tsp ground turmeric (*serbuk kunyit*)

1 large tomato, seeded and cut into
2-cm ($^{3}/_{4}$-in) cubes

60 ml (2 fl oz / $^{1}/_{4}$ cup) yoghurt

70 g ($2^{1}/_{2}$ oz) green peas

Salt to taste

Ground white pepper to taste

1 fresh green chilli, seeded and cut
into 2-cm ($^{3}/_{4}$-in) pieces

2 sprigs coriander (cilantro), roughly
chopped

1. Prepare *rempah*. Place all ingredients in a food processor and grind into
a paste.

2. Prepare filling. Heat oil in a wok or medium saucepan over medium heat.
Fry cardamoms, star anise, cinnamon and curry leaves until aromatic.

3. Add onion and sauté until soft. Add ginger and garlic paste and continue
cooking for 1 minute before adding in the chicken. Cook until the meat
turns opaque.

4. Add water. Add *rempah*, carrot, ground spices (coriander, fennel,
turmeric) and tomato. Mix well. Bring to a boil over medium heat.

5. Stir in the yoghurt and mix well. Add green peas. Season with salt and
pepper to taste. Toss in the green chilli and coriander leaves and mix
well. Allow filling to cool down overnight for the flavours to develop.

6. Preheat oven to 180°C (350°F) for at least 10–15 minutes.

7. **To assemble:** Using a slotted spoon, scoop filling into a 20 cm (8 in)
deep pie dish to two-thirds full.

8. Spread potato slices over the filling. Brush potato topping with egg wash
using a pastry brush.

9. Bake for 40–45 minutes or until the potato is golden brown.

10. Top with fried curry leaves.

# Ayam Masak Merah Pot Pie

Family: Serves 5–6 • Personal: Makes five 10 x 5-cm (4 x 2-in) pies

Traditionally eaten at Malay weddings, this well-loved specialty
is also served during the Malay fasting month of Ramadhan. Our version of this
pot pie sees the addition of aromatics like lemongrass, turmeric and galangal to the spice paste.
Fried chicken is simmered in a delicious crimson sauce that's sweet and spicy from
tomato and chilli with coconut milk for a creamy finish.

1 egg, lightly beaten for egg wash

**PASTRY**

Atta shortcrust, Plain shortcrust,
  Phyllo, Puff

**REMPAH**

3 Tbsp fried chilli paste (sambal *tumis*)
  (page 26)

Thumb-size ginger, peeled and sliced

Double-thumb size galangal (*lengkuas*),
  peeled and sliced

2 stalks lemongrass (*serai*), white
  portion, sliced

Thumb-size turmeric, peeled and sliced

2-cm (³/₄-in) piece shrimp paste
  (*belacan*) or 1 tsp *belacan* powder

10 medium shallots, peeled and sliced

2 cloves garlic, peeled and sliced

**FILLING**

600 g (1 lb 5¹/₃ oz) chicken meat,
  cut into 2-cm (³/₄-in) cubes

1¹/₂ tsp salt + more to taste

1 tsp ground turmeric (*serbuk kunyit*)

105 ml (3¹/₂ fl oz / 7 Tbsp) oil

1 clove garlic, peeled and minced

10 medium shallots, peeled and diced

400 g (14¹/₃ oz) canned tomatoes,
  chopped, juice reserved

3 Tbsp tomato paste

250 ml (8 fl oz / 1 cup) coconut milk
  (*santan cair*)

125 ml (4 fl oz / ¹/₂ cup) coconut cream
  (*santan pekat*)

sugar to taste

1. Prepare *rempah*. Place all ingredients in a food processor and grind
   into a paste.

2. Prepare filling. Season chicken with salt and ground turmeric for
   30 minutes.

3. Heat 4 tablespoons oil in a wok or medium saucepan over high heat.
   Fry the chicken until light brown. Drain on kitchen towels and set aside.

4. Add remaining oil into the wok and sauté garlic and shallots until soft
   and aromatic.

5. Add canned tomatoes and juice. Stir until well incorporated into the garlic
   and shallot paste.

6. Add *rempah* and continue to cook until it reaches *pecah minyak*.

7. Add coconut milk. Lower the heat and let chicken simmer for at least
   10 minutes before adding in the coconut cream. Cook until the gravy
   thickens. Season with salt and sugar to taste.

8. Allow curry to cool down overnight for the flavours to develop before
   baking.

9. Preheat the oven to 180°C (350°F) for 10–15 minutes.

10. **To assemble**: Roll out the dough between 2 pieces of silicon baking
    sheets or onto a lightly floured surface to a 3 mm (¹/₈ in) thickness,
    with about 5 cm (2 in) in excess of the pie dish or casing. Trim excess
    dough and set trimmings aside.

11. Spoon filling into the dish to about two-thirds full. Cover the filling with
    the dough. Using a cookie cutter of your choice, cut shapes using pastry
    trimmings to decorate the pie. Brush pie top with egg wash using a
    pastry brush.

12. Create steam holes by making a small cross in the pie top using the tip
    of a knife. Crimp pie edges as desired. Bake for 50–60 minutes or until
    golden brown.

    NOTE: If using store-bought spice paste, 3¹/₂ tablespoons suffices. Add it in step 6.

$\mathcal{T}$ip Slice a whole block of shrimp paste, toast in
a small oven toaster. Allow to cool and grind into a
powder form. Store in a jar. Powdered shrimp paste is
available in major supermarkets.

# Indonesian Opor Ayam Pot Pie

Personal: Makes 5 pies

Growing up in Malaysia, I used to look forward to extended family gatherings in Singapore where meals would conjure memories of delicious curries cooked by my late *Popo* (grandma) who hails from Indonesia. *Opor ayam* cooked with freshly ground coriander is one of my favourite curries from her treasure trove of Indonesian specialties.

1 egg, lightly beaten for egg wash

**PASTRY**
Cumin shortcrust, Plain shortcrust, Puff

**REMPAH**
3 cloves garlic, peeled and sliced

2 slices galangal (*lengkuas*), peeled and coarsely chopped

Thumb-size ginger knob, peeled and coarsely chopped

4 candlenuts (*buah keras*)

1 tsp ground cumin (*serbuk jintan putih*)

1 tsp ground fennel (*serbuk jintan manis*)

3 tsp ground coriander (*serbuk ketumbar*)

1 tsp ground black pepper

**FILLING**
600 g (1 lb 5$^1$/$_3$ oz) chicken meat, diced into 3-cm (1$^1$/$_5$-in) cubes

125 ml (4 fl oz / $^1$/$_2$ cup) oil

20 medium shallots, peeled and thinly sliced to deep-fry

2 stalks lemongrass (*serai*), white portion bruised with a cleaver

5 cm (2 in) cinnamon stick

2 large onions, peeled and diced

155 ml (5$^1$/$_5$ fl oz / $^3$/$_5$ cup) coconut milk (*santan cair*)

1 Tbsp tamarind water (*asam jawa*) or $^1$/$_2$ Tbsp lemon juice

2 kaffir lime leaves (*daun limau purut*)

2 bay leaves (*daun salam*)

$^1$/$_2$ tsp salt

1 tsp sugar

300 g (10$^1$/$_2$ oz) baby potatoes, parboiled 10 minutes and thickly sliced

1. Prepare *rempah*. Place all ingredients in a food processor and grind into a paste.

2. Prepare filling. Season the chicken with *rempah* for 30 minutes. Meanwhile, heat oil in a wok or medium saucepan over medium heat and deep-fry the shallots until golden brown. Using a slotted spoon, remove the fried shallots and drain on paper towels.

3. In the same wok or saucepan, add lemongrass and cinnamon and stir-fry for 5 minutes in the remaining oil. Add the onions and sauté until soft.

4. Add marinated chicken and cook until the meat turns opaque. Add coconut milk. Add the tamarind water or lemon juice, kaffir lime leaves and bay leaves. If you're using lemon juice, add it in the last 5 minutes of cooking.

5. Reduce heat to low and simmer chicken for 15 minutes, then cook until the meat is tender.

6. Season the curry with salt and sugar to taste. Allow filling to cool down overnight for the flavours to develop before baking.

7. Preheat the oven to 180°C (350°F) for at least 10–15 minutes.

8. **To assemble:** Line the sides and base of terracotta pots with sliced potatoes. Spoon filling into each pot to about two-thirds full. Sprinkle half a teaspoon of fried shallots on top of the filling before covering it with dough.

9. Roll out the dough between 2 pieces of silicon baking sheets or onto a lightly floured surface to a 3 mm ($^1$/$_8$ in) thickness, with about 5 cm (2 in) in excess of the pie dish or case.

10. Press dough firmly onto the rim. Trim excess dough and set trimmings aside.

11. Create steam holes by making a small cross in the pie top using the tip of a knife. Decorate pie top with trimmings as desired. Brush pie top with egg wash using a pastry brush.

12. Bake for 40–45 minutes or until golden brown.

NOTE: To prepare tamarind water, see page 140. Alternatively, use 1–2 tablespoons of store-bought tamarind paste.

# Satay Chicken Pie

Personal: Makes five 13 x 3-cm ($5^1/_{10}$ x $1^1/_5$-in) pies

This pie, shaped like a kidney, is in honour of my beloved late mother, a former midwife.
She makes the best satay I've ever tasted. Like many Asian women who
employ their instincts when cooking, her recipe was totally committed to memory.
She gleaned precious tips from her Malay patients on making a good satay great.
The meat would come from free-range chickens raised in our backyard.
My siblings and I would skewer the satay while my dad would then charcoal-grill the meat.
The combined aromas of spice-marinated satay sizzling over smoking-hot charcoal ambers
and caramelised sugar from the meat drippings are simply inviting.

1 egg, lightly beaten for egg wash
cucumber wedges, as needed
sliced onions, as needed

**PASTRY**
Atta shortcrust, Plain shortcrust, Puff

**REMPAH**
10 medium shallots, peeled and diced
2 cloves garlic, peeled and sliced
2-cm ($^3/_4$-in) ginger, peeled and sliced
2 stalks lemongrass (*serai*), white
portion only, sliced
Thumb-size galangal (*lengkuas*),
peeled and sliced
Half thumb-size turmeric, peeled
and sliced

**FILLING**
500 g (1 lb $1^1/_2$ oz) chicken meat
$1^1/_2$ Tbsp sugar
$1^1/_2$ Tbsp ground coriander
(*serbuk ketumbar*)
1 Tbsp ground fennel (*serbuk
jintan manis*)
1 Tbsp ground cumin (*serbuk
jintan putih*)
Salt to taste
1 stalk lemongrass (*serai*), white
portion, bruised with a cleaver
2 Tbsp oil

1. Prepare *rempah*. Place all ingredients in a food processor and grind into a paste.

2. Prepare filling. In a medium mixing bowl, marinate chicken with sugar for 30 minutes. Add *rempah*, ground spices and water if required. Mix until meat is well coated with the marinade and refrigerate overnight.

3. Prepare satay sauce. Place garlic, onions, lemongrass, galangal, turmeric, shrimp paste and dried red chillies in a food processor and grind into a paste. Transfer ground ingredients to a small mixing bowl.

4. Heat oil in a wok or small saucepan, fry the satay sauce and *rempah* and stir until it reaches *pecah minyak*. Add ground peanut and tamarind water. Season with salt and palm sugar to taste. Set aside until ready to serve.

5. Turn on the oven grill. Place chicken steaks onto a baking tray, basting it using a bruised lemongrass stalk dipped in oil. When meat has cooled down, cut into 1-cm ($^1/_2$-in) cubes.

6. Preheat oven to 180°C (350°F) for at least 10–15 minutes.

7. **To assemble:** For the bottom crust, roll out the dough between 2 pieces of silicon baking sheets or on a lightly floured surface to a 3 mm ($^1/_8$ in) thickness, with about 5 cm (2 in) in excess of the pie trays. Line the tray with bottom pastry, trimming the excess dough. Dock using a fork. Fill kidney-shape pie trays with grilled chicken. Cover with top pastry.

8. Crimp pastry edges with the back of a fork. Create steam holes by making a small cross using the tip of a knife. Brush pie top with egg wash using a pastry brush.

9. Bake for 40–45 minutes or until golden brown. Drizzle satay sauce in between the groves of the pie.

10. Serve with cucumber and sliced onions.

NOTE: If using store-bought paste, $3^1/_2$ tablespoons suffices. Add it in step 2.

## SATAY SAUCE

- 2 cloves garlic, peeled
- 4 large onions, peeled and roughly chopped
- 4 stalks lemongrass (*serai*), white portion, sliced
- Thumb-size galangal (*lengkuas*), peeled and sliced
- Thumb-size turmeric (*kunyit*), peeled and sliced
- 3 Tbsp oil
- 1 tsp ground shrimp paste (*belacan*)
- 14 dried red chillies, seeded, softened in water
- 150 g (5 oz) roasted peanuts, skinned and coarsely ground
- 1 Tbsp tamarind pulp mixed with 375 ml (12 fl oz / 1½ cups) water
- Salt to taste
- 4 Tbsp palm sugar (*gula Melaka*) or to taste

*Tip* Cook the satay sauce the day before for flavours to develop overnight. If a silky smooth sauce is preferred, substitute with creamy peanut butter.

*Tip* Garlic and ginger paste is sold separately in jars at Indian groceries.

# Butter Chicken Pot Pie

Family: Serves 4–5 • Personal: Makes 5 pies

The first time I tasted butter chicken was in New Delhi, in a nondescript restaurant. It was absolutely delicious! And at subsequent meals for the rest of my India trip, butter chicken was what I ate, or rather what I only wanted to eat! This recipe belongs to Suja, a great cook who demonstrated how to prepare this dish at a dinner party that I attended. This version of butter chicken contains unique nutty accents with the addition of ground cashew nuts.

1 egg, lightly beaten for egg wash

**PASTRY**
Atta shortcrust, Plain shortcrust,
  Yoghurt shortcrust

**MARINADE**
$^3/_4$ tsp salt
1 tsp ground white pepper
25 g (1 oz) curd or yoghurt
Thumb-size turmeric (*kunyit*), grated

**SPICE PASTE**
100 g ($3^1/_2$ oz) butter
$^3/_4$ tsp chilli powder
5 tomatoes, diced
5 onions, peeled and diced
25 g (1 oz) cashew nuts, ground
$1^1/_2$ tsp garlic paste
$1^1/_2$ tsp ginger paste

**FILLING**
500 g (1 lb $1^1/_2$ oz) chicken meat,
  cut into 3-cm ($1^1/_5$-in) cubes
5 cm (2 in) cinnamon stick (*kayu manis*)
2 cardamoms (*buah pelaga*), bruised
3 cloves (*bunga cengkih*)
2 bay leaves (*daun salam*)
1 Tbsp oil
2 Tbsp fenugreek leaves (*daun halba*)
2 sprigs coriander leaves (cilantro), minced
Salt to taste
Ground white pepper to taste
1 tsp jaggery (Indian palm sugar)
60 ml (2 fl oz / $^1/_4$ cup) canned cream
  or heavy cream
25 g (1 oz) butter

1. Prepare marinade. In a medium mixing bowl, rub salt, pepper, curd or yoghurt and turmeric into the chicken to marinate the meat for 30 minutes.

2. Prepare spice paste. Place butter into a saucepan and fry chilli powder, tomato, onions, cashew nuts and garlic and ginger paste together. Allow to cool and then grind into a paste in a food processor.

3. Prepare filling. Place cinnamon, cardamoms, cloves and bay leaves in a muslin bag and tie tightly. Heat oil in a medium saucepan and add chicken and spice paste.

4. Simmer until chicken is tender, then add fenugreek and coriander leaves. Season with salt, ground white pepper and jaggery to taste.

5. Add cream and butter, then mix it into the chicken until well incorporated. Simmer for 5 minutes. Allow the filling to cool down overnight for the flavours to develop before baking.

6. Preheat the oven to 180°C (350°F) for at least 10–15 minutes.

7. **To assemble:** Roll out the dough between 2 pieces of silicon baking sheets or on a lightly floured surface to a 3 mm ($^1/_8$ in) thickness, with about 2 cm ($^3/_4$ in) in excess of the pie dish.

8. Spoon curry into pie dish to two-thirds full. Cover the filling with pastry. Trim excess dough and set trimmings aside.

9. Using a cookie cutter of your choice, cut shapes using pastry trimmings to decorate the pie. Create steam holes by making a small cross in the pie top using the tip of a knife. Crimp pie edges with the back of a fork.

10. Bake for 40–45 minutes until golden brown.

NOTE: If using store-bought spice paste, $3^1/_2$ tablespoons suffices.
  Add it in step 3.

# Beggar's Chicken

Makes 1 portion serving 5–6

The origins of this dish tells of a stolen chicken, hastily wrapped in mud to conceal a theft, then thrown in an open fire. It turned out to be one of Chinese's greatest culinary innovations. Our version of this Chinese classic that originates in Hangzhou, China is triple wrapping a well-seasoned tender spring chicken with lotus leaf, greaseproof paper and finally pastry to create a "Dutch oven" effect for succulent results.

1 kg (2 lb 3 oz) whole chicken, wing tips removed
500 ml (16 fl oz / 2 cups) oil
1 dried lotus leaf, scalded in boiling water to soften
1 sheet greaseproof paper
1 egg, lightly beaten for egg wash

**PASTRY**
Five-spice shortcrust

**MARINADE**
Thumb-size ginger, peeled
12 shallots, peeled
5 cloves garlic, peeled
2 tsp salt
2 tsp sugar
1 Tbsp light soy sauce
1/2 Tbsp oyster sauce
2 tsp sesame oil
1 Tbsp ginger juice
1 Tbsp Chinese Shaoxing wine
1 Tbsp brandy (optional)
2 Tbsp oil
2 Tbsp water
1/2 Tbsp cornflour
A pinch of ground white pepper

*Tip* **If Chinese Shaoxing wine is unavailable, substitute with dry sherry.**

1. Prepare marinade. Using a food processor, grind ginger, shallots and garlic into a paste. Alternatively, you may also pound ingredients using a mortar and pestle. Place in a large mixing bowl together with remaining marinade ingredients and mix well.

2. Brush the chicken with the marinade using a pastry brush. Pour the extra marinade into the chicken cavity. Place chicken in the refrigerator and let stand for at least 5 hours, preferably overnight for the flavours to develop.

3. Drain the chicken of excess marinade. Truss the chicken legs with kitchen string. Heat oil in a wok or saucepan. When oil is hot, deep-fry the chicken until golden brown, basting it with the hot oil. Remove and set aside to cool.

4. To prepare the lotus leaf, cut off tip at the top of the softened leaf. Pat leaf dry using paper towels.

5. Prepare sauce. Mix all ingredients in a small bowl. Heat a small saucepan over low heat. Pour the sauce in a saucepan and stir with a wooden spoon until the sauce thickens.

6. Meanwhile, preheat the oven to 150°C (300°F) for at least 10–15 minutes.

7. **To assemble:** Lay the greaseproof paper onto a baking tray. Place the lotus leaf on top of it and position the chicken in the centre with its breast facing up.

8. First, wrap the whole bird up snugly with the lotus leaf into a parcel, followed by a second wrapping using the greaseproof paper. This prevents the juices from oozing out during baking.

9. Next, roll out the dough to a 3 mm (1/8 in) thick pastry sheet, making sure it is large enough to cover the chicken. Place the wrapped chicken at the centre and wrap the entire chicken with the pastry. Seal the ends by crimping the pastry together. Trim excess pastry.

10. Transfer to a baking tray. Using a sharp knife, score a line 5 cm (2 in) beyond the circumference of the pastry. This makes it easy to cut off the top crust after baking.

11. Brush dough with egg wash using a pastry brush. Bake at 150°C (300°F) for 1.5 hours. This allows the heat to penetrate the chicken and cook it thoroughly. Increase the heat to 170°C (340°F) and continue baking for another 1 hour until pastry is golden brown. Remove from oven and let it stand for 10 minutes.

    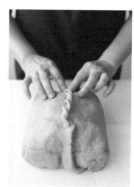

## SAUCE

8 Tbsp water or chicken stock

2 tsp sugar

1/2 tsp salt

3 tsp soy sauce

1–2 tsp dark soy sauce

1 1/2 tsp sesame oil

2 tsp cornflour

A pinch of ground white pepper

1 tsp brandy (optional)

12. Using the tip of a sharp knife, trace the scored line on the top crust and cut it out. Gently remove the wrapped chicken and place on a serving platter. Unwrap the paper, followed by the lotus leaf.

13. Serve chicken portions with a drizzle of the sauce and pastry.

NOTE: Lotus leaves vary in size. Choose one that is large enough to wrap the whole chicken. Trim off the excess.

*Tip* Store-bought tamarind paste is available in major supermarkets. Mix 2 tablespoons with 125 ml (4 fl oz / ¹/₂ cup) water.

# Nyonya Ayam Buah Keluak Pot Pie

Personal: Makes 9 pies

This dish is probably the culinary icon of Straits Chinese (Peranakan) cuisine.
The Indonesian black nut, *buah keluak*, is what characterizes the umami dimension
of this intriguing dish, 'revered' by the Peranakans. Simmered in a spicy tamarind sauce scented
with coriander, galangal and other spices, the tender chicken filling makes a palatable pie.
This recipe is courtesy of Aunt Tan Kiah Whee.

1 Tbsp ground coriander
(*serbuk ketumbar*)

1 egg, lightly beaten for egg wash

### PASTRY
Puff, Plain shortcrust

### REMPAH
2 Tbsp fried chilli paste
(sambal *tumis*) (page 26)

8 cloves garlic, peeled

20 medium shallots, peeled and sliced

Double-thumb size galangal (*lengkuas*),
peeled and sliced

Thumb-size turmeric (*kunyit*), peeled
and sliced

2 stalks lemongrass (*serai*), white
portion only, sliced

1 Tbsp dried shrimp paste (*belacan*)
(optional)

### FILLING
4 Tbsp oil

600 g (1 lb 5$^1$/$_3$ oz) chicken meat,
diced into 3-cm (1$^1$/$_5$-in) cubes

50 g (1$^2$/$_3$ oz) tamarind pulp
(*asam jawa*), mixed with 125 ml
(4 fl oz / $^1$/$_2$ cup) water

100 g (3$^1$/$_2$ oz) Indonesian black nut
meat extract (*buah keluak*), mixed
with 1 tsp salt

Salt to taste

2 tsp sugar

1. Prepare *rempah*. Place all ingredients into a food processor and grind to a paste.

2. Transfer *rempah* to a small mixing bowl. Mix in the ground coriander until it is well incorporated.

3. Prepare filling. Heat oil in a wok or medium saucepan over medium heat. Sauté the *rempah*, stirring continually until it reaches *pecah minyak*.

4. Add chicken and cook until the meat turns opaque and is evenly coated with the *rempah*.

5. Add tamarind water to cover the chicken. Reduce to low heat and simmer until the meat is tender. Add *buah keluak* paste and stir in until well incorporated.

6. Season with salt and sugar to taste. Allow filling to cool down overnight for the flavours to develop before baking.

7. Preheat the oven to 180°C (350°F) for at least 10–15 minutes.

8. **To assemble:** Spoon filling into a Chinese tea cup or pie dish to about two-thirds full. Roll out the dough between 2 pieces of silicon baking sheets or onto a lightly floured surface to a 3 mm ($^1$/$_8$ in) thickness and 5 cm (2 in) larger than the circumference of pie dish. Using a lattice roller, cut the rolled out pastry with it. Trim it to the diameter of the pie dish. Using your fingers, slowly pull it outwards until the lattice opens up. Give pie top an egg wash using a pastry brush.

9. Bake for 40–45 minutes or until golden brown.

10. Serve within 30 minutes while the pastry is crisp.

# Thai Roast Duck Red Curry Pot Pie

Personal: Makes 3 pies

A well-roasted duck, done the Chinese way, with five spices is
*de rigeur* to a lip-smacking red curry pie. The mild acidity of honey pineapple
and the citrusy scent of kaffir lime leaves are the perfect counterfoils
to the creaminess of coconut milk. But first, you have to chomp
through the crisp buttery shortcrust pastry.

1 egg, lightly beaten for egg wash

**PASTRY**

Atta shortcrust, Plain shortcrust,
    Flaky, Puff

**FILLING**

80 g (2⁴/₅ oz) home-made red curry
    paste (page 27, alternatively use
    store-bought paste)

2 Tbsp water

250 ml (8 fl oz / 1 cup) coconut milk
    (*santan cair*)

2 kaffir lime leaves (*daun limau purut*)

150 g (5 oz) round aubergines
    (eggplants), cut into large cubes

4 canned pineapple rings, cut into
    8 wedges

15 cherry tomatoes (a mixture of red,
    yellow and orange)

200 g (7 oz) Chinese roast duck breast
    meat, cut into 2-cm (³/₄-in) cubes

1 Tbsp Thai palm sugar or brown sugar

3 long red chillies, seeded and sliced
    into 1-cm (¹/₂-in) lengths

A handful of Thai basil leaves

1. Prepare filling. Combine red curry paste with water. Place red curry paste, coconut milk and kaffir lime leaves in a medium pot and cook over medium heat. Bring to a slow boil and cook for about 15 minutes until the oil separates.

2. Add round aubergines, pineapple wedges and tomatoes. Cook for 5 minutes. Add duck meat and cook for a further 5 minutes over low heat. Season with Thai palm sugar or brown sugar. Toss in red chillies and Thai basil leaves. Mix until well incorporated.

3. Allow filling to cool down before baking.

4. Preheat the oven to 180°C (350°F) for at least 10–15 minutes.

5. **To assemble**: Roll out the dough between 2 pieces of silicon baking sheets or onto a lightly floured surface to a 3 mm (¹/₈ in) thickness, with about 5 cm (2 in) in excess of the 15 x 5 cm (6 x 2 in) pie dish or case.

6. Spoon filling into the dish to about two-thirds full. Cover the filling with puff pastry. Trim excess dough and set trimmings aside. Create steam holes by making a small cross in the pie top using the tip of a knife. Crimp pie edges as desired. Using a cookie cutter, cut shapes using pastry trimmings to decorate the pie top. Brush pie top with egg wash using a pastry brush.

7. Bake for 40–50 minutes or until golden brown.

    NOTE: If using store-bought spice paste, 3 tablespoons suffices. Add it in step 1.

*Tip* To release the fragrance of kaffir lime leaves, crush them in the palm of your hand.

# Masala Turkey and Cranberry Chutney Pie

Family: Serves 4

Let this Masala Turkey Pie take pride of joy at the Christmas dining table.
Layered with a spiced cranberry chutney and baked with yoghurt pastry, serve piping hot
with a chilled cucumber raita. Turkey never tasted this good at Christmas!

500 g (1lb 1½ oz) turkey breast, halved and butterflied

1 Tbsp melted ghee

1 egg, lightly beaten for egg wash

## PASTRY

Atta shortcrust, Plain shortcrust

## CUCUMBER RAITA

1 medium Japanese cucumber, seeded and cut into cubes

1 clove garlic, peeled and finely minced

2 shallots, peeled and finely minced

2 Tbsp mint leaves, finely shredded

1 small red chilli, seeded and diced (optional)

2 Tbsp yoghurt

Salt to taste

## CRANBERRY CHUTNEY

120 g (4¼ oz) dried cranberries

125 ml (4 fl oz / ½ cup) orange juice

60 g (2 oz) sugar

¾ tsp mixed spices or ground cinnamon

## YOGHURT MARINADE

1 Tbsp salt

1 Tbsp ginger paste

1 Tbsp garlic paste

1 Tbsp lemon juice

1 tsp beetroot juice

1½ tsp ground coriander

1½ tsp ground

1 tsp BBQ tandoori garam masala or normal garam masala

1 tsp Kashmiri red chilli powder

1½ tsp fresh turmeric (kunyit) paste

250 ml (4 fl oz / 1 cup) yoghurt, preferably Greek-style

1. Prepare cucumber raita. In a medium mixing bowl, mix *raita* ingredients and chill in the fridge.

2. Prepare cranberry chutney. Combine all ingredients in a small saucepan and cook over low heat, stirring continually until the dried fruit becomes sticky. Prepare the chutney a day ahead of baking.

3. Prepare yoghurt marinade. In a medium mixing bowl, rub turkey with salt, ginger paste and garlic paste. Add remaining marinade ingredients and marinate for 30 minutes.

4. Preheat oven grill. Grill turkey for 25–30 minutes, checking periodically to prevent the turkey from burning. Flip turkey over and brush with melted ghee. Return to the oven to bake until cooked. Let cooked turkey rest for 5 minutes, then shred thickly.

5. Roll out the dough between 2 pieces of silicon baking sheets or on a lightly floured surface. Cut out 8 rectangular pieces measuring 19 x 7.5-cm (7.5 x 3-in). Line a baking tray with silicon baking sheet.

6. Preheat oven to 180°C (350°F) for at least 10–15 minutes.

7. **To assemble:** Lay four pieces of rectangular pastry lengthwise at right angles to one another — at 12 o'clock, 3 o'clock, 6 o'clock and 9 o'clock. For the remaining pastry, lay each rectangle in between two (e.g. 12 o'clock and 3 o'clock) pieces of dough until you get a total of 8 rectangles.

8. Lay turkey meat onto each piece of pastry in a clockwise manner, starting from 12 o'clock to resemble a ring. Spread with a layer of cranberry chutney. Put another layer of turkey meat over the chutney.

9. Picking up the dough at the shorter end, fold inwards to cover the filling. Gently tuck under the bottom dough to hold it in place. Repeat until all the filling is covered. Decorate pie top with cut-outs from pastry trimmings using cookie cutters of your choice.

10. Brush with egg wash using a pastry brush. Bake for 40–45 minutes or until golden brown. Allow it to stand for 15 minutes before serving with a cucumber raita.

NOTE: If Kashmiri chilli powder is unavailable, substitute with paprika.

# Seafood

Sardine and Chilli Puffs 86

Malaysian Muar Otah Parcels 89

Gulai Ikan in Pastry 90

Penang Asam Laksa Puffs 93

Singapore Chilli Crab Mini Puffs 94

Sambal Petai Prawn Mini Pies 97

Baked Crab with Pastry Crown 98

Thai Tom Yam Soup with Pastry Crown 101

Seafood Laksa Lemak Pie 102

# Sardine and Chilli Puffs

Personal: Makes 12 puffs

My maiden attempt at making sardine puffs during my school-going days
using a square contraption with an open base (ingeniously called an 'oven')
and placed over a gas stove proved to be a trying affair. The whole process
took so long that I served them for lunch instead of breakfast.
This version, with curry leaves pressed into the pastry is *shiokadoo!*

1 egg, lightly beaten for egg wash

**PASTRY**

Flaky, Plain shortcrust, Yoghurt
  shortcrust, Puff

**FILLING**

425 g (15 oz) canned sardines in
  tomato sauce

6 large calamansi limes, juiced

1/2 tsp salt

1 tsp sugar

60 ml (2 fl oz / 1/4 cup) oil

2 medium onions, peeled and
  thinly sliced

3 medium red chillies, seeded
  and thinly sliced

3 medium green chillies, seeded
  and thinly sliced

2 Tbsp tomato paste

1 sprig curry leaves, stalks removed
  and shredded

1. Prepare filling. In a medium mixing bowl, coarsely mash the sardines using a fork, including the bones if preferred. Mix lime juice with salt and sugar and set aside.

2. Heat oil in a wok or medium saucepan over medium heat. Sauté the onions until soft. Toss in the red and green chillies and continue to cook for another 30 seconds.

3. Add tomato paste and mashed sardines. Mix until just combined. Allow the filling to cool down before baking.

4. Preheat the oven to 180°C (350°F) for at least 10–15 minutes.

5. **To assemble:** Knead the curry leaves into the dough and roll it out between 2 pieces of silicon baking sheets or on a lightly floured surface to a 3 mm (1/8 in) thickness. Using 10 cm (4 in) round cookie cutters, cut out pastry circles, two pieces per puff. Place 2 1/2 tablespoons filling in the centre of the pastry, fold it over and pleat to seal the edges. Chill for 10 minutes before baking. Repeat until the filling is used up.

6. Brush each puff with egg wash using a pastry brush.

7. Bake for 20 minutes or until golden brown.

# Malaysian Muar Otah Parcels

Personal: Makes 8 parcels

These parcels of *otah* (spiced fish paste) are a cinch to make.
All you need are two key ingredients: good Muar *otah*,
reputably Malaysia's best and puff pastry. If you want a peppery accent,
sandwich the *otah* with wild pepper leaves, then wrap up and
into the oven they go for 15 minutes.

1 egg, lightly beaten for egg wash

**PASTRY**
Flaky, Puff pastry, 2 sheets
    24 cm (9½-in) pastry squares

**FILLING**
2 packets 180 g (6 oz) fish *otah*
8 wild pepper leaves (optional)

*Tip* Fish *otah* can be substituted with prawn or *sotong otah*.

1. Preheat the oven to 190°C (370°F) for at least 10–15 minutes. Meanwhile, cut each *otah* while frozen into 2 pieces.

2. Remove two puff pastry sheets straight from the freezer. Cut into four square pieces, each measuring 8-cm (⅓-in). Set aside trimmings to decorate the pie top.

3. **To assemble:** If using flaky pastry, roll out the dough between 2 pieces of silicon baking sheets or onto a lightly floured surface to a 3 mm (⅛ in) thickness. Sandwich each piece of *otah* between 2 pieces of pepper leaves, if using, and then place it in the centre of the pastry square. Using a pastry brush dipped in water, brush along the rim of the pastry. Bring each corner of the pastry to the centre and press along the rims to seal the pastry. Using a leaf cutter, cut out 4 pastry leaves and lay them over the joints. Make small pastry rosettes for the centre of each parcel.

4. Give each parcel an egg wash using a pastry brush. Bake for 15 minutes or until golden brown.

# Gulai Ikan in Pastry

Family: Makes 2 pies

Watch the reactions of your dining guests as this fish-shaped pie takes centre stage on the dining table. Unlike the Western counterpart that's often creamy, our version is a tasty fish curry that's been cooked with a flavourful spice paste. Shaping the pastry is a fairly simple process that's totally fun. Looks and tastes yummy too!

1 egg, lightly beaten for egg wash

**PASTRY**
Puff

**REMPAH**
10 shallots, peeled and diced

6 cloves garlic, peeled

Thumb-size turmeric (*kunyit*), peeled and roughly chopped

Thumb-size ginger, peeled and diced

Thumb-size galangal (*lengkuas*), peeled and sliced

1 Tbsp ground coriander (*serbuk ketumbar*)

3–4 Tbsp fried chilli paste (sambal *tumis*) (page 26)

**FILLING**
60 ml (2 fl oz / ¼ cup) oil

2 stalks lemongrass (*serai*), white portion, bruised

500 ml (16 fl oz / 2 cups) coconut milk (*santan cair*)

3 bay leaves

1 fresh turmeric leaf (*daun kunyit*)

3 tamarind peels (*asam keping*) or 2 Tbsp tamarind paste*

500 g (1 lb 1½ oz) fish meat (mackerel), cut into 3-cm (1⅕-in) cubes

1 tsp salt

1 Tbsp sugar

1. Prepare *rempah*. Place shallots, garlic, turmeric, ginger and galangal in a food processor and grind into a paste. In a small mixing bowl, mix blended ingredients with ground coriander and sambal *tumis* until well mixed.

2. Prepare filling. Heat oil in a wok or medium saucepan over medium heat. Fry lemongrass for 1 minute, then add *rempah* and cook until it reaches *pecah minyak*.

3. Add coconut milk, bay leaves, turmeric leaf and tamarind peels or tamarind paste. Reduce heat to low and allow the gravy to simmer for 20 minutes.

4. Add fish and cook until the meat turns white. Season with salt and sugar to taste. Turn heat off immediately. Allow the filling to cool down before baking. Discard lemongrass, bay leaves, turmeric leaf and tamarind peels.

5. Preheat the oven to 190°C (370°F) for at least 10 minutes.

6. **To assemble:** Using a fish-shaped template, trace the outlines using greaseproof paper.

7. Remove the store-bought puff pastry from the freezer. Place the traced outline over the pastry and cut out the fish shape. Spoon filling over the pastry body of the fish and refrigerate it. Meanwhile, cut out 4-cm (1½-in) pastry circles, about 20–25 pieces. Cut out two pieces of fish-shaped pastry to form the top and bottom crusts. Lay pastry circles over the top pastry, overlapping them until the whole fish is covered.

8. Brush pie with egg wash using a pastry brush.

9. Bake for 40–45 minutes or until golden brown.

   *NOTE: To prepare tamarind water, see page 140. Alternatively, use 1–2 tablespoons of store-bought tamarind paste.

*Tip* Replace a pinch of salt with 2 drops of lemon juice.

# Penang Asam Laksa Puffs

Makes 8 puffs

My palate tingles with excitement every time I smell *asam* laksa. I first had home-made *asam* laksa at Penangnite Shu's place and her spicy hot version wow-ed my palate. With an aromatic, piquant and tangy sourish-sweetish fish broth, this Malaysian specialty is a scrumptious infusion of flavours that uses fresh aromatics like laksa leaves, lemongrass and ginger torch bud.

1 egg, lightly beaten for egg wash

**PASTRY**
Puff

**DIAMOND-SHAPE TEMPLATES**
18 x 11 cm (7 x 4²/₅ in); 15 x 9 cm (6 x 3¹/₂ in)

**FILLING**
500 ml (16 fl oz / 2 cups) water

2 stalks lemongrass (*serai*), white portion bruised with a cleaver

Thumb-size galangal (*lengkuas*), thickly sliced and bruised

1 sprig laksa leaves (*daun kesom*) or Vietnamese mint leaves, stalk and vein removed

1 small torch ginger bud (*bunga kantan*), halved

¹/₂ honey pineapple, skinned, eyes removed or 4 pineapple rings cut into 2-cm (³/₄-in) cubes

200 g (7 oz) *asam* laksa paste

500 g (1 lb 1¹/₂ oz) fish meat extracted from 1 kg (2 lb 3 oz) horse mackerel (*ikan kembong*) or mackerel (*ikan selar*), steamed

**GARNISH**
¹/₂ cucumber, seeded and finely diced

1 pineapple ring, diced into 0.5-cm (¹/₄-in) cubes

1 small red onion, peeled and finely diced

¹/₂ ginger torch bud (*bunga kantan*), finely diced

1 red chilli, seeded and finely diced

2 sprigs fresh mint, finely shredded

2 Tbsp Penang shrimp paste, diluted with 1 Tbsp of reserved fish stock

1. Prepare filling. In a medium saucepan, bring water to a boil. Add lemongrass, galangal, laksa or Vietnamese mint leaves, torch ginger bud, honey pineapple and 50 g (1²/₃ oz) *asam* laksa paste. Reduce heat and simmer for 30 minutes until aromatic.

2. Increase the heat and bring to a boil. Add fish, reduce heat and poach gently for 15 minutes or until cooked. Remove the fish and set it aside to cool. When cooled, flake the meat coarsely, taking care to discard the fine fish bones.

3. Strain the stock, discarding the fresh herbs (lemongrass, galangal, torch ginger bud and laksa leaves). Reserve 1–2 tablespoons stock for the shrimp paste.

4. In a medium mixing bowl, gently mix cooked fish with remaining *asam* laksa paste and the fish stock for a moist filling.

5. Preheat the oven to 180°C (350°F) for at least 10–15 minutes.

6. **To make diamond-shaped pastry shells:** Using the larger diamond-shape template, cut out 8 pieces of pastry. Transfer them onto 2 baking sheets, 4 per sheet. Repeat until all pastry shells are assembled. Brush top pastry with egg wash using a pastry brush.

7. Using the tip of a knife, score a line 1 cm (¹/₂ in) from the edge of the diamond. Blast chill in the freezer for 15–20 minutes.

8. Bake for 20 minutes or until golden brown and puffed up. Remove from the oven. Carefully remove each lid, cutting along the scored line. Allow them to cool for 15 minutes.

9. **To assemble:** Scoop 2 tablespoons of filling into each pastry shell, top with a sprinkling of the garnish and a drizzle of the shrimp paste.

# Singapore Chilli Crab Mini Puffs

Makes 20 mini puffs

Chilli crab is hugely popular in Singapore. Every weekend,
Singaporeans chow down kilos of chilli crab at seafood restaurants across the island.
Tucking into the delicate meat of the crustacean tossed in a sweet and sour chilli
and tomato-based sauce can get messy. Instead, enjoy them as bite-sized tartlets.

1 Chinese coriander (cilantro),
   finely chopped, for garnishing

**PASTRY**
Puff

**FILLING**
2 Tbsp oil

2 cloves garlic, peeled and finely
   minced

Thumb-size knob ginger, peeled
   and finely minced

200 g (7 oz) chilli crab paste

200 g (7 oz) crab meat or crab sticks,
   cut into 1-cm (1/2-in) pieces

1 small egg, lightly beaten

1 spring onion (scallion), white portion
   only, thinly sliced. Set aside green
   leaves for garnishing

1. Prepare filling. Heat oil in a wok or small saucepan. Sauté the garlic
   and ginger for 2 minutes until aromatic. Add chilli crab paste and cook
   for 5 minutes, stirring continually until well mixed.

2. Add crab meat or crab sticks and cook for 1 minute. Using a fork, whisk in
   beaten egg, stirring continually until the egg coagulates. Turn off the heat
   immediately. Toss in the sliced spring onions and stir through.

3. Preheat oven to 175°C (340°F) for at least 10–15 minutes.

4. **To make the mini puff shells**: If store-bought vol-au-vents (mini puff
   shells) are not available, make your own. Using a round 4.5 cm (1⁴/₅ in)
   cutter, cut out round discs. Using a 3 cm (1¹/₂ in) cutter, cut rings from
   the pastry. Put away the centres. Dip your finger in water and rub along
   the entire edge of the larger dough, then lay the ring on top of it. Pat top
   dough lightly so that it sticks to the bottom piece. Repeat until all pastry
   shells are assembled. Brush pastry with an egg wash using a pastry brush.

5. Bake for 10–15 minutes until golden brown and puffed up.

6. **To assemble:** Fill each shell to the brim. Garnish with finely chopped
   coriander and spring onions. Serve immediately.

Tip For a less pungent flavour, blanch stink beans in boiling water for 2 minutes and drain it.

# Sambal Petai Prawn Mini Pies

*Makes 20 mini pies*

Sarah and I debated whether *petai* and pastry would make tasty pies.
I cooked my late mother's version of her sambal *petai* tossed in a deliciously spicy
home-made sambal with dried shrimps that has been pan-fried to a light crisp.
Our panel of tasters polished them up with gusto!

1 egg, lightly beaten for egg wash

**PASTRY**

Flaky, Plain shortcrust, Yoghurt
   shortcrust, Puff

**REMPAH**

Thumb-size galangal (*lengkuas*),
   peeled and sliced

4 stalks lemongrass (*serai*),
   white portion, sliced

25 medium shallots, peeled and
   sliced finely

2 cloves garlic, peeled and minced

6 Tbsp fried chilli paste
   (sambal *tumis*) (page 26)

2 tsp shrimp paste powder
   (*serbuk belacan*)

2 Tbsp water

**FILLING**

200 ml (6³/₄ fl oz / ³/₄ cup) oil

100 g (3¹/₂ oz) dried prawns (*haebee*),
   soaked in hot water for 5 minutes,
   drained and coarsely diced

300 g (10¹/₂ oz) small prawns,
   shelled and deveined

180 g (6 oz) stink beans (*petai*),
   peeled and roughly diced

1 tsp tamarind pulp (*asam jawa*)
   mixed with 2 Tbsp water

¹/₂ tsp salt

1 tsp sugar

1. Prepare *rempah*. Place galangal, lemongrass, shallots and garlic in a food processor and grind into a paste. In a medium mixing bowl, mix sambal *tumis* and *belacan* with water to a paste until both are incorporated. Alternatively, using a mortar and pestle, pound hard ingredients first, starting with galangal, lemongrass, garlic, adding the belacan powder last and mixing it to a paste with the water.

2. Prepare filling. Heat oil in a wok or medium saucepan over medium heat. Add *rempah* and cook until it reaches *pecah minyak*. Set aside.

3. Fry dried prawns to a light crisp. Drain on paper towels and set aside. Toss in fresh prawns and stir-fry for 2 minutes.

4. Toss in the stink beans and reduce to low heat. Mix in the fried dried prawns. Cook for another 10 minutes. Add tamarind water. Cook the mixture until thick. Season with salt and sugar to taste. Allow the filling to cool down before baking.

5. Preheat the oven to 180°C (350°F) for at least 10–15 minutes.

6. **To assemble:** Roll out the dough between 2 pieces of silicon baking sheets or on a lightly floured surface to 3 mm (¹/₈ in) thickness.

7. Using a round ring cutter, cut out pastry circles with a circumference of 9-cm (3¹/₂-in). Spoon 2 tablespoons filling onto each piece of dough. Cover the filling with another piece of dough. Press both pastry layers (top and bottom) together. Pleat the edges to seal the pie.

8. Use a heart-shape cookie cutter (or any other cutter) cut out heart-shapes and paste them onto the pie top. Brush pie top with egg wash using a pastry brush.

9. Bake for 40–45 minutes until golden brown.

# Baked Crab with Pastry Crown

Makes 7–8 individual portions

Sarah's version of this classic Cantonese dish is an adaptation of her mother's recipe.
Her mom would serve this delicacy whenever crab was available in the morning wet market.
In this recipe, delicate crabmeat is pepped up with minced prawn and pork for a meatier,
robust stuffing. For textural contrast, Sarah added a pastry crown to the stuffed crab.

oil, as needed

1 egg, lightly beaten for egg wash

**PASTRY**
Flaky, Puff

**SAUCE**
250 ml (4 fl oz / 1 cup) water

1/2 tsp salt

2 Tbsp sugar

4 Tbsp tomato sauce

1 tsp Worcestershire sauce

1 Tbsp sesame oil

2 tsp curry powder

1 Tbsp cornflour, mixed with
   a little water

**FILLING**
2 Tbsp oil

1 large onion, peeled and sliced

225 g (8 oz) prawn meat, minced

150 g (5 oz) minced pork

1 egg

1 tsp salt

1/2 tsp sugar

1 tsp light soy sauce

1 tsp sesame oil

Ground white pepper to taste

6 crabs: 150 g (5 oz) crabmeat,
   retain empty crab shells

15 g (1/2 oz) Chinese dried mushrooms,
   diced into 1-cm (1/2-in) cubes

20 g (1 oz) ham, sliced into strips

1 Tbsp cornflour

1. Prepare sauce. In a small saucepan, mix all ingredients together except
   for cornflour. Bring to a boil over medium heat. Add cornflour solution
   to thicken the sauce.

2. Prepare filling. Heat oil in a wok or medium saucepan over medium heat.
   Sauté onion until soft and set aside.

3. In a large mixing bowl, mix prawn and pork together. Crack in the egg.
   Add salt, sugar, light soy sauce, sesame oil and pepper. Add crabmeat,
   Chinese mushrooms and ham. Mix until well-blended. Add sautéed onions
   and mix in the cornflour to obtain a sticky paste.

4. Preheat oven to 180°C (350°F) for at least 10–15 minutes.

5. **To assemble:** Clean crab shell and spoon in the filling to two-thirds full.
   Remove puff pastry from the freezer. Cut the pastry to fit the size of the
   crab shell with a 3 mm (1/8 in) in excess to cover the filling. Press the
   edges together to seal it. Trim excess dough and set it aside.

6. Grease a baking tray with oil before placing the filled crabs on it. Using a
   cookie cutter of your choice, cut pastry trimmings to decorate each crab.
   Brush pie top with egg wash using a pastry brush.

7. Bake until pastry is golden brown. Serve piping hot with a drizzle
   of the sauce.

# Thai Tom Yam Soup with Pastry Crown

Makes 4 portions

I just love how *tom yum goong* (prawns in a spicy tangy soup) perks up my
palate with its assertive notes—hot, sour, fiery, briny and citrusy.
It may look bland but it's so flavoursome from the infusion of aromatics like lemongrass,
coriander roots, kaffir lime leaves and galangal. Enjoy it piping hot with a puff pastry crown.

1 egg, lightly beaten for egg wash

fresh Thai coriander, for garnish

**PASTRY**
Puff

**FILLING**
375 ml (12 fl oz / 1¹/₂ cups) chicken stock

2 slices galangal (*lengkuas*)

2 stalks lemongrass (*serai*), white portion, bruised with a cleaver

5 stalks coriander roots, bruised

2 kaffir lime leaves (*daun limau purut*), roughly torn

5 Tbsp tom yam paste

5 bird's eye chillies (chilli *padi*), (You may reduce if you prefer the tom yam to be less spicy.)

300 g (10¹/₂ oz) fresh medium prawns, shelled and deveined

100 g (3¹/₂ oz) canned straw mushrooms, drained and halved

1¹/₂ Tbsp lemon juice (optional)

1 tsp fish sauce, optional if using ready-made Thai tom yam paste

1. Prepare filling. Heat chicken stock in a medium saucepan over medium heat. Add galangal, lemongrass, coriander roots and kaffir lime leaves. Reduce heat to low and simmer for 15 minutes.

2. Add tom yam paste and chilli *padi*, if using. Simmer for another 15 minutes.

3. Bring stock to a slow boil. Add fresh prawns and mushrooms, then cook for 5 minutes. Add lemon juice if a tangy soup is preferred. Taste and add fish sauce if required. Turn off heat and allow soup to cool down.

4. Preheat the oven to 180°C (350°F) for at least 10–15 minutes.

5. **To assemble**: Roll out the dough between 2 pieces of silicon baking sheets or on a lightly floured surface to a 3 mm (¹/₈ in) thickness, with about 2 cm (³/₄ in) in excess of the pie bowl.

6. Place on a baking tray to bake the pastry separately. Create steam holes by making a small cross using a knife. Brush with egg wash using a pastry brush.

7. Bake for 15–20 minutes or until golden brown.

8. Cover the bowl with the pastry crown. Garnish with fresh Thai coriander.

# Seafood Laksa Lemak Pie

Personal: Makes 5–6 pies

Who can resist a fragrant laksa? The spice paste is a powerhouse of perfumes and flavours with aromatics like kaffir lime, laksa leaves, torch ginger bud and lemongrass. The milky coconut stock is creamy, sweet, rich and flavoursome from the seafood cooked in it. This pie is so indulgent when paired with freshly baked pastry.

6 paper cases 11 x 2.5 cm (4⁴/₅ x 1 in), with small holes

1 egg, lightly beaten for egg wash

### PASTRY

Plain shortcrust, Puff

### POACHING LIQUID

375 ml (12 fl oz / 1½ cups) coconut milk (*santan pekat*)

4 Tbsp laksa *rempah* (page 26 or store-bought spice paste)

1 stalk lemongrass (*serai*), white portion, bruised

Thumb-size galangal (*lengkuas*), peeled and bruised with a cleaver

2 kaffir lime leaves (*daun limau purut*)

1 small torch ginger bud (*bunga kantan*), halved

2 sprigs laksa leaves (*daun kesom*) or Vietnamese mint leaves, discard stalks

300 g (10½ oz) prawn heads and shells, pan-fried in 2 Tbsp oil with 2 cloves bruised garlic

1¼ tsp salt

### FILLING

250 g (9 oz) salmon fillet, cut into 2-cm (³/₄-in) cubes

300 g (10½ oz) prawns, shelled and deveined, cut into 1-cm (½-in) cubes

150 g (5 oz) fishcakes, cut into 1-cm (½-in) cubes

70 g (2½ oz) tofu puffs, cut into 2-cm (³/₄-in) cubes

Roux: 1 Tbsp oil + 1 Tbsp flour

1 small torch ginger bud, finely shredded

3 sprigs laksa leaves (*daun kesom*) or Vietnamese mint leaves, discard stalks and finely shredded

1 kaffir lime leaf, finely shredded and vein removed

1. Prepare poaching liquid. In a medium saucepan over low heat, combine poaching liquid ingredients. Simmer gently for 10 minutes.

2. Prepare filling. Add salmon, prawns, fishcakes and tofu puffs to saucepan containing poaching liquid. Poach gently for 2 minutes, then sieve the seafood. Transfer to a medium mixing bowl. Keep the poaching liquid simmering over very low heat. Discard the solids.

3. In a separate medium saucepan, heat oil and toss in the flour. Cook until it thickens, then add poaching liquid, half a cup at a time, stirring continually until all the liquid is used up and it begins to thicken. Add seafood and stir gently. Toss in finely shredded torch ginger, 2 sprigs laksa or Vietnamese mint leaves and kaffir lime leaf.

4. Allow filling to cool down overnight for the flavours to develop before baking.

5. Preheat oven to 190°C (370°F) for at least 10–15 minutes.

6. **To assemble:** Roll out shortcrust dough between 2 pieces of silicon baking sheets or on a lightly floured surface to a 3 mm (¹/₈ in) thickness. Line 5–6 personal pie cases with bottom pastry. Spoon filling to two-thirds full.

7. Finely shred remaining laksa or Vietnamese mint leaf and sprinkle some over the filling before covering with puff pastry. Trim excess dough. Crimp the edges as desired. Using a cookie cutter of your choice, decorate pie top with cut outs from the trimmings. Brush pie top with egg wash using a pastry brush.

8. Bake for 20 minutes or until golden brown. Serve piping hot.

*Tip* If candlenuts are unavailable, substitute with macadamia nuts.

# Vegetarian

Japanese Vegetarian Pot Pie 106

Sweet Potato Tart with Spicy Mayo 109

Cauliflower and Keema Lattice Pie 110

Golden Pumpkin Bon Bon 113

# Japanese Vegetarian Pot Pie

Family: Serves 4–5 • Personal: Makes 4

This curry pie has Japanese, Indian and Italian flavours rolled into one.
To call it a curry is somewhat a misnomer. While it has hints of Indian spices,
the pie cannot be labelled as a bona fide curry as it is fruity and sweet from
the tomato paste and tonkotsu sauce. It tastes more like a stew and yet is not
quite a stew. Nonetheless, it makes a tasty vegetarian pie.

1 egg, lightly beaten for egg wash

**PASTRY**

Flaky, Plain Shortcrust, Puff

**FILLING**

2 Tbsp oil

1 large onion, peeled and diced

1 medium potato, peeled and thinly
  sliced using a mandolin

1 Tbsp curry powder

375 ml (12 fl oz / 1$^1$/$_2$ cups) water

150 g (5 oz) Japanese pumpkin, skinned
  and diced into 2-cm ($^3$/$_4$-in) cubes

1 medium Fuji apple, peeled, cored
  and grated

2 tsp Japanese rice wine (mirin)

1 Tbsp tomato paste

1 Tbsp tonkotsu sauce

Roux: 1 tsp flour mixed with +
  1 tsp water to form a paste

90 g (3 oz) Japanese soy beans
  (edamame), shelled

1 tsp salt

1 tsp sugar

1. Prepare filling. Heat oil in a wok or medium saucepan. Sauté onion until soft. Toss in the potato. Sprinkle the curry powder over the potato and continue frying.

2. Add 250 ml (8 fl oz / 1 cup) water. Reduce to low heat and simmer potato until tender but still firm, then add pumpkin cubes.

3. Add freshly grated apple to the stew, followed by mirin. Cook the curry for another 10–15 minutes.

4. Add tomato paste, tonkotsu sauce, roux, followed by the edamame. Allow the curry to simmer until it starts to thicken. Season with salt and sugar to taste.

5. Allow filling to cool down overnight for the flavours to develop before baking.

6. Preheat oven to 180°C (350°F) for at least 10–15 minutes.

7. **To assemble:** Spoon filling into 4 individual bowls. Cut a sheet of 24-cm (9$^1$/$_2$-in) pastry square into four pieces. Cover each bowl with a pastry square and trim edges. Create steam holes by making a small cross in the pastry using the tip of a knife.

8. Brush pie top with egg wash using a pastry brush. Bake for 30–40 minutes or until golden brown.

*Tip* Substitute pumpkin with Japanese sweet potato.

*Tip* The orange sweet potato cooks faster than the yellow and purple cultivars. In order to get the same texture from all three colours remove the orange sweet potatoes once they are cooked.

# Sweet Potato Tart with Spicy Mayo

Makes 1 sweet potato tart that serves 4

Sweet potato comes in a selection of colours that will make
a visually appealing savoury tart. Serve it with a soothing mayo
to temper the masala-marinated potatoes.

1 egg, lightly beaten for egg wash

## PASTRY
One sheet 24 cm (9$^{1}/_{2}$ in) square
   puff pastry

## FILLING
1 kg (2 lb 3 oz) sweet potatoes
   (yellow, orange and purple),
   peeled and soaked in water with
   a pinch of salt added

1 tsp garam masala

$^{1}/_{2}$ tsp chilli flakes (optional)

1 tsp toasted cumin seeds (*jintan putih*)

2 sprigs parsley, finely minced

2 Tbsp yoghurt

1 tsp salt

2 Tbsp ghee

## SPICY MAYO
60 ml (2 fl oz / $^{1}/_{4}$ cup) mayonnaise

1 tsp honey

2 tsp tobasco sauce or sweet chilli
   sauce

1. Prepare filling. Parboil sweet potatoes in a deep saucepan. Remove the orange ones after 17 minutes. Continue cooking the purple and yellow sweet potatoes for another 3 minutes. Drain and rinse sweet potatoes quickly with cold water. Allow it to cool for 5 minutes.

2. Using a sharp knife, cut sweet potatoes into 4-cm (1$^{1}/_{2}$-in) slices of 3-mm ($^{1}/_{8}$-in) thickness. Discard any slices that are smaller than 4 cm (1$^{1}/_{2}$ in).

3. In a deep mixing bowl, blend together garam masala, chilli flakes, if using, cumin seeds, parsley, yoghurt, salt and ghee until well incorporated.

4. Toss sweet potatoes in the spice mixture until evenly coated.

5. Preheat oven to 180°C (350°F) for at least 10–15 minutes.

6. Place one sheet of 24 cm (9$^{1}/_{2}$ in) pastry square onto a baking tray. Arrange sweet potato slices over it, alternating with different colours to close up any gaps.

7. Bake for 30–40 minutes until puffed up and golden brown.

8. Prepare spicy mayo. In a mixing bowl, mix all ingredients together.

9. Cut into slices and serve piping hot, adding more spicy mayo if desired.

# Cauliflower and Keema Lattice Pie

Family: Makes one 20-cm (8-in) pie that serves 5 • Personal: Makes 5 pies

Keema is a traditional South Asian dish that has its roots in Persian cuisine.
Typically cooked with minced meat (usually mutton), potatoes and peas, Mahes' vegetarian
version has the vitamin C-packed cauliflower and green peas simmered in a sauce infused
with spices like mustard seeds and fennel for an equally delicious keema.

1 egg, lightly beaten for egg wash

**PASTRY**
Atta shortcrust, Plain shortcrust, Puff

**FILLING**
$^1/_2$ tsp mustard seeds (*biji sawi*)

1 tsp ground fennel (*serbuk jintan manis*)

2 large onions, peeled and diced

4 medium potatoes, peeled and diced into 2-cm ($^3/_4$-in) cubes

Thumb-size ginger, peeled and blend together with 2 cloves garlic to get 1 Tbsp of paste

Water, as needed

1 medium carrot, peeled and diced into 2-cm ($^3/_4$-in) cubes

190 g ($6^4/_5$ oz) cauliflower, cut into small florets

1 tsp ground turmeric (*serbuk kunyit*)

2 tsp chilli powder

155 g (5 oz) green peas

Salt to taste

3 sprigs curry leaves, discard stalks

1 Tbsp lemon juice

1. Prepare filling. Heat a wok or medium saucepan over medium heat. Toast the mustard seeds until you hear a cracking sound. Reduce the heat, then toss in the fennel and continue frying until fragrant.

2. Toss in the onions to sauté until soft. Add potatoes, blended garlic and ginger paste. Stir-fry for half a minute, then add enough water to cover the potatoes. Bring to a boil over high heat. Reduce heat and simmer over medium heat until potatoes are half-cooked. Add carrot and cauliflower. Stir-fry for 1 minute. Add turmeric, chilli powder and green peas.

3. Season with salt to taste. Continue to simmer until gravy thickens before adding the curry leaves and lemon juice. Allow filling to cool down overnight for the flavours to develop before baking.

4. Preheat oven to 180°C (350°F) for at least 10–15 minutes.

5. **To assemble:** Roll out the dough between 2 pieces of silicon baking sheets or onto a lightly floured surface to a 3 mm ($^1/_8$ in) thickness. Cut the pastry into 2-cm ($^3/_4$-in) and 1-cm ($^1/_2$-in) strips long enough to cover the diameter of the pie dish. Cover the filling, leaving a 2 cm ($^3/_4$ in) gap between each strip. Interweave the strips to form a lattice pattern. If the dough gets too soft, chill in the fridge until it firms up.

6. Brush pie top with egg wash using a pastry brush.

7. Bake for 40 minutes or until golden brown.

*Tip* An easier way is to form the lattice on a sheet of baking paper 5 cm (2-in) larger than the pie dish. Cut pastry into 1-cm ($^1/_2$-in) long pieces, leaving a 2 cm ($^3/_4$ in) gap between the strips. Interweave the remaining strips to form a lattice pattern. Chill in the fridge until firm. Slowly, lay the entire piece of lattice pastry over the filling and remove the baking paper. Trim excess pastry.

# Golden Pumpkin Bon Bon

Personal: Makes 16

The sweet flavours of the saffron-coloured pumpkin intensify with baking.
Sarah pre-cooks the pumpkin with umami-laced Chinese mushrooms,
steams it before slicing and then wraps it in phyllo pastry before baking.

125 ml (4 fl oz / ¹/₂ cup) melted butter

**PASTRY**

1 sheet of Phyllo pastry, cut into
25 x 20-cm (10 x 8-in) to yield
16 pieces

**FILLING**

3 Tbsp oil + more as needed

1 large onion, peeled and diced

2 Chinese dried mushrooms, soaked
until softened and cut into 2-cm
(³/₄-in) cubes

Salt to taste

Ground white pepper to taste

350 ml (11⁴/₅ fl oz / 1¹/₂ cups) water +
more as needed

350 g (12 oz) pumpkin, peeled and
diced into 3-cm (1¹/₅-in) cubes

250 g (8 oz) rice flour

*Tip* Make the pumpkin
filling the night before baking.

1. Prepare filling. Heat oil in a wok or medium saucepan over medium
   heat. Sauté onion until aromatic before adding in Chinese mushrooms.
   Continue to fry for 1 minute. Season with salt and pepper to taste.
   Set mushrooms aside.

2. In the same saucepan, add water before adding the pumpkin. Allow it
   to boil over medium heat until soft. Using a fork, mash the pumpkin.

3. In a medium mixing bowl, add rice flour, then add just enough water
   to dissolve it until it resembles a runny paste. Stir the mixture into the
   mashed pumpkin and mix well until incorporated. Add to mushroom
   mixture. The texture of the batter should be thick and not watery.

4. Using a 19 cm (9 in) square tray, oil the base and sides of the tin. Spoon
   in the pumpkin batter and steam for 1 hour or until it becomes firm.

5. Allow it to cool down before refrigerating it overnight.

6. Preheat oven to 180°C (350°F) for at least 10–15 minutes.

7. **To assemble:** Cut chilled pumpkin into 5-cm (2-in) squares. Brush each
   piece of phyllo with melted butter. Lay another piece of phyllo on top
   and brush with melted butter. Place one pumpkin piece in the centre.
   Wrap the phyllo around the pumpkin. To secure the filling, twist both
   ends to resemble a sweet or bon bon; using your fingers, gently open up
   the pastry. Repeat until all the pumpkin is used up.

8. Grease a baking tray with melted butter before putting the pumpkin bon
   bon onto it. Brush pastry sheets evenly with melted butter.

9. Bake until golden brown and crispy. Serve piping hot.

   NOTE: To check if the pumpkin is cooked, insert a satay stick into the centre
   of the pumpkin. If it comes out clean, the pumpkin is cooked.

# Desserts

# Apple Rosette Tart

Family: Makes one 27-cm (11⁴/₅-in) pie that serves 8

This luxurious looking apple pie is perfect for Mother's Day.
Our version is an adaptation of the classic French Apple Tart where the
accent is on the fruit. Sweet and juicy fresh apple is sliced and
creatively assembled into a beautiful rosette. Present it to her freshly baked.
It will surely warm Mom's heart and maybe bring on a few tears too!

1 egg, lightly beaten for an egg wash

**PASTRY**
Sweet pastry
430 g (15 oz) plain (all-purpose) flour
40 g (1¹/₂ oz) icing sugar
185 g (6¹/₂ oz) cold butter, diced into
   1-cm (¹/₂-in) cubes
2 egg yolks
2–3 Tbsp chilled water

**FILLING**
4 large green apples, peeled, cored
   and sliced
120 g (4¹/₅ oz) castor sugar
5 cm (2 in) cinnamon stick
A pinch of ground nutmeg
2 Tbsp water
35 g (1 oz) pineapple jam
30 g (1 oz) butter

**APPLE ROSETTE CROWN**
4 red Fuji apples, skinned, cored and
   thinly sliced
1 Tbsp pineapple jam, mixed with
   a little hot water for a glaze

*Tip* For evenly thin apple
slices, use a mandolin. Soak sliced
apples in a large mixing bowl of
water with a few drops of lemon
juice added to prevent the fruit
from oxidising.

1. Prepare pastry. In a large bowl, mix flour, icing sugar and butter together.
   Add egg yolks and incorporate them well using a fork, adding chilled
   water 1 tablespoon at a time until it forms a dough.

2. Knead for a few minutes until the flour stops sticking to the fingers.
   Pat into a disc, wrap with cling film and chill for 30 minutes

3. Prepare filling. In a large saucepan, place apple, castor sugar, cinnamon,
   ground nutmeg and water. Cover and cook over medium heat until apple
   slices turn soft. Turn off the heat and sieve excess liquid. Transfer to a
   medium mixing bowl. Add pineapple jam and butter. Mix evenly and set
   aside to cool. Discard cinnamon and cloves.

4. Preheat oven to 180°C (350°F) for at least 10–15 minutes.

5. **To assemble:** Divide the dough into 2 portions. Wrap with cling film and
   refrigerate for 30 minutes. Freeze the second portion for another tart.

6. Take 1 portion of the dough out from the fridge. Roll out between
   2 pieces of silicon baking sheets or onto a lightly floured surface to a
   3 mm (¹/₈ in) thickness.

7. Press the dough firmly to the base and side of the pie dish. Trim off any
   excess dough. Blind bake the bottom crust for 15 minutes. Remove from
   oven and let it cool. Spoon cooked apple filling over the bottom pastry
   until two-thirds full.

8. **To assemble the apple rosette crown:** Start arranging sliced apples
   from the outside in concentric circles, overlapping slightly and working
   your way towards the centre in a clockwise direction until you get a
   rosette heart.

9. Bake for 25 minutes or until apple turns soft. Remove the tart from the
   oven and brush with pineapple glaze using a pastry brush.

# Mango Tart

Makes four 10-cm (4-in) individual tarts

Coconut mango, so named for its round shape and orange meaty flesh
is ideal for this *yummilicious* tart. The succulent fruit, weighing in at over 1 kg from
Bee Chan's mango tree contrasts beautifully with the nutty crunch from the macadamia nut brittle.
A drizzle of kaffir lime sauce adds flourish and perks up the tropical flavours.

Oil or melted butter, as needed

4 tsp brown sugar

2 kaffir lime leaves, spines removed
and finely shredded

2 mangoes, ripe yet firm, skinned
and sliced

1 egg, lightly beaten for an egg wash

100 g macadamia nut brittle,
roughly chopped

Vanilla ice cream, to serve (optional)

**PASTRY**
Puff

**KAFFIR LIME SAUCE**

4 tsp brown sugar

2 Tbsp butter

2 Tbsp water

1 kaffir lime leaf, torn into pieces

*Tip* Substitute macadamia
nut brittle with peanut brittle
if unavailable.

1. Prepare kaffir lime sauce. In a small saucepan, place brown sugar, butter and water over medium heat. Let it come to a slow boil, then toss in kaffir lime leaf. Turn heat off immediately. Discard kaffir lime leaf. Set aside.

2. Preheat oven to 190°C (370°F) for at least 10–15 minutes.

3. Grease four shallow ramekins, each measuring 10 x 2.5 cm (4 x 1 in) with an oil spray or brush with melted butter using a pastry brush.

4. Sprinkle a teaspoon of brown sugar over the base of each ramekin. Using a blowtorch, direct the heat to cook until the sugar turns light brown. Sprinkle with kaffir lime leaves, then line with mango slices.

5. Using ring cutters, cut out pastry circles 1-cm (1/2-in) beyond the ramekin's circumference.

6. Lay the pastry over the mango and tuck the excess into the edges of the ramekin.

7. Brush dough with egg wash using a pastry brush. Create steam holes by making a small cross in the pie top using the tip of a knife.

8. Bake for 20–25 minutes until golden brown. After 2 minutes, invert tarts onto dessert plates. Sprinkle with chopped macadamia nut brittle and drizzle with kaffir lime sauce. Serve with vanilla ice cream if preferred.

# Durian Tartlets

Makes 32 tartlets

During one durian party, Sarah turned leftover durian into delectable durian tartlets.
Making them requires just one simple step— cream is whipped into the durian pulp —
then piped into store-bought ready-made cases that have been heated up to a crisp.

**PASTRY**

32 store-bought sweet shortcrust
   tartlet cases

**FILLING**

350 g (12 oz) durian pulp
150 g (5 oz) whipping cream

 Separate the durian pulp
from the seeds and store them in
an air-tight container. Freeze until
ready to use.

1. Bake store-bought tartlet cases in the oven at 160°C (320°F) until the
   buttery aroma wafts from the oven. Remove the tartlet cases and let
   them cool down.

2. Prepare filling. Whisk durian pulp together and whipping cream together
   in a food processor until smooth.

3. Spoon filling into a piping bag and pipe it into the tartlet cases.
   Refrigerate until ready to serve.

# Upside Down Banana Tart

Makes one 26 x 13-cm (10 x 5-in) *tranche* tart serving 8–10

In Asia, bananas are often eaten as *goreng pisang* (deep-fried banana fritters)
during tea-time. When I got a bunch of freshly harvested bananas from Bee Chan's garden,
I made this tasty tart. The contrast in textures between the crisp biscuit base, sweet banana,
and palm sugar salted caramel is accentuated with creamy ice cream.

4–5 ripe bananas (preferably
*pisang rajah*), peeled and
halved lengthwise

1 egg, lightly beaten for egg wash

Ice cream of your choice

Orange sanding sugar, as needed

**PASTRY**
Puff

**GULA MELAKA SALTED CARAMEL**
30 g (1 oz) palm sugar
(*gula melaka),* chopped

75 g (2¹/₂ oz) white sugar

2 Tbsp water

2 pandan leaves, knotted

185 ml (6 fl oz / ³/₄ cup) coconut milk
(*santan cair*)

1 tsp glutinous rice flour, mixed
with 1 tsp water to form a paste

1 tsp salt

1. Prepare *gula melaka* salted caramel. Place palm sugar, white sugar, water and pandan leaves in a small saucepan and cook until sugar dissolves. Add coconut milk and simmer for 2 minutes, stirring continuously.

2. In a small mixing bowl, mix the glutinous rice paste and salt together. Slowly add it to palm sugar mixture and mix until well-blended. Turn off heat and discard the pandan leaves. Cool down before using.

3. Spoon half the *gula melaka* salted caramel into the base of the tart pan. Place the bananas side by side over the caramel.

4. Preheat the oven to 190°C (370°F) for at least 10–15 minutes.

5. **To assemble:** Cover the banana with pastry and tuck the excess into the edges of the pie dish.

6. Brush dough with egg wash using a pastry brush. Create steam holes by making a small cross in the pie top using the tip of a knife.

7. Bake for 40–45 minutes or until golden brown. When baked, leave the tart in the pan to cool down. Invert onto a rectangular plate.

8. Serve hot with a scoop of ice cream drizzled with *gula melaka* salted caramel, if desired.

9. Sprinkle with orange sanding sugar, if desired.

NOTE: The mixture will bubble and splatter when coconut milk is added.

# Chocolate and Chilli Tart

Makes one 20-cm (8-in) tart

Chilli and chocolate are great bed-fellows. The fiery heat of the chilli adds
a zing to the dense rich flavours of dark chocolate before it gets an injection of rum.
They come together beautifully on the palate, converting skeptics into
fans of this delectably decadent dessert.

Oil or melted butter as needed

**BISCUIT BASE**

225 g (8 oz) black biscuits, remove
icing or chocolate pastry (page 25)

1 Tbsp butter, melted

**GANACHE**

150 g (5 oz) dark chocolate, chopped
into small pieces

30 g (1 oz) butter

2 tsp sugar

85 ml (2¹/₂ fl oz / ¹/₃ cup) double cream

1 bird's eye chilli (chilli *padi*), seeded
(optional)

A pinch of sea salt

2 tsp rum (optional)

**PEANUT BRITTLE TOPPING**

35 g (1 oz) peanut brittle, roughly
chopped (optional)

60 g (2 oz) wholegrain wheat biscuits,
crushed

1¹/₂ Tbsp butter, melted

**MANGO-PASSIONFRUIT COULIS**

4 Tbsp orange juice

3 Tbsp mango purée

2 passionfruits, pulp only

¹/₂ tsp cornflour

2 tsp sugar

1¹/₂ tsp butter

1. Preheat the oven to 180°C (350°F) for at least 10–15 minutes. Grease a 23 cm (9 in) tart tin.

2. Prepare biscuit base. Using a mortar and pestle, crush biscuits until they become crumbs. Alternatively, you may also grind biscuits using a food processor.

3. In a medium bowl, mix biscuits with melted butter. Press mixture onto the base of the tart tin. Refrigerate.

4. Prepare ganache. Place the dark chocolate into a medium mixing bowl and set aside. In a small saucepan, mix butter, sugar, double cream and chilli *padi* over medium heat until it begins to bubble. Remove from the heat. Discard the chilli and sprinkle sea salt into the mixture. Add rum, if using. Pour the cream mixture over the chocolate. This will melt the chocolate. Mix until well-blended. Allow to cool down.

5. Pour the ganache over the biscuit base. Refrigerate until the filling is set.

6. Prepare peanut brittle topping. Grind peanut brittle and wholegrain wheat biscuits in a food processor until they become crumbs. Mix with butter in a small bowl. Sprinkle over the ganache.

7. Prepare mango-passionfruit coulis. Place orange juice, mango purée, passionfruit pulp, cornflour and sugar in a small saucepan. Cook over low heat until the sugar melts and thickens. Fold in the butter until it is well incorporated. Set coulis aside to cool. Drizzle it over the tart before serving.

NOTE: If using chocolate pastry, roll out and blind bake for 15 minutes until cooked. Allow pastry to cool down before filling with ganache.

*Tip* Use chocolate with 70% cocoa butter for a robust cocoa flavour.

# Assorted Nut Tartlets

Makes 58 tartlets

This is definitely for nut lovers! The melange of cashew nuts and
assorted seeds with fragrant spices plus a hint of pepper is so seductive!
Finely shredded lemongrass and kaffir lime leaves are tossed into the
whole mixture which is then bound together with salted caramel.

7.5 cm (3 in) boat-shaped tart tins

**PASTRY**
250 (9 oz) butter
70 g (2$^1/_2$ oz) castor sugar
60 g (2$^1/_4$ oz) icing sugar
350 g (12 oz) plain (all-purpose) flour
110 g (4 oz) cornflour
40 g ground almonds
$^1/_2$ tsp vanilla extract
1 small egg, lightly beaten

**FILLING**
40 g (1$^1/_4$ oz) cashew nuts,
  roughly chopped
2 Tbsp pine nuts
33 g (1 oz) pumpkin seeds
2 Tbsp melon seeds
1 Tbsp black sesame seeds
1 Tbsp white sesame seeds
1 tsp toasted cumin seeds
  (*jintan putih*)
$^1/_4$ tsp freshly ground black pepper
2 Tbsp palm sugar (*gula melaka*)
50 g (1$^2/_3$ oz) white sugar
2 Tbsp water
1 kaffir lime leaf (*daun limau purut*),
  stalk and middle vein removed,
  finely minced
2 stalks lemongrass (*serai*), white
  portion, finely minced
1 tsp butter
1 tsp sea salt

1. Prepare pastry. In a deep mixing bowl, using your fingers, rub butter into the dry ingredients until it resembles breadcrumbs. Pour in the egg and mix until it forms a dough.

2. Wrap dough with cling film and flatten into a disc. Refrigerate for 30 minutes or put in the freezer for 15 minutes.

3. Preheat oven to 180°C (350°F) for at least 10–15 minutes.

4. **To assemble:** Remove dough from the fridge. Wait for a few minutes for dough to soften. Press it into the base and sides of 7.5 cm (3 in) boat-shaped tart cases. Trim excess dough.

5. Blind bake tart cases for at least 10 minutes until light brown. Allow to cool before using.

6. Prepare filling. Spread cashew nuts, pine nuts, pumpkin seeds, melon seeds, black and white sesame seeds and cumin seeds on a baking tray and toast in the oven for 5 minutes. Remove tray to stir the nuts before returning it to the oven to bake for another 5 minutes. Transfer to a bowl and sprinkle with black pepper. Mix well.

7. Meanwhile, combine palm sugar and white sugar, water, kaffir lime leaf and lemongrass in a small saucepan over medium low heat and cook until sugars dissolve and thicken. Add butter and let it melt before adding the sea salt. Turn off the heat. Stir in the nut mixture, working quickly to coat nuts with the palm sugar.

8. Spoon 2 tsp nut filling into each pastry case. Chill tartlets in the fridge until set before serving.

# Tropical Fruit Tart

*Makes one 26 x 13-cm (10 x 5-in) tranche tart that serves 8–10*

There's no shortage of fresh tropical fruits to make this easy-to-please tart.
The choice of fruit is entirely up to you. Everything about this
tart is so tropical, from the biscuit base to citrus-scented pastry cream
that supports the assortment of fresh fruit. Great as a family tart or as *petit-fours*!

Oil or melted butter as needed

### PASTRY CREAM
65 g (2¼ oz) granulated sugar
38 g (1 oz) cornflour
A pinch of salt
500 ml (16 fl oz / 2 cups) milk
4 egg yolks
1 tsp orange extract
30 g (1 oz) butter, chilled and
   cut into cubes

### ORANGE TART PASTRY
240 g (8½ oz) plain (all-purpose) flour
   + more as needed
50 g (1²⁄² oz) castor sugar
150 g (5 oz) butter
¼ tsp salt
1 tsp vanilla extract, mixed with
   1 Tbsp cold water
1 orange, zest only
1 egg

### ASSORTED FRUITS
Mango
Dragon fruit
Rambutan
Pineapples
Banana

### GLAZE
2 Tbsp pineapple jam
6 Tbsp water

*Tip* When the pastry cream
coats the back of the wooden
spoon, remove from heat.

1. Prepare pastry cream. Mix sugar, cornflour and salt together in a medium saucepan. In a deep mixing bowl, beat milk, egg yolks and orange extract together. Slowly pour into the dry ingredients and whisk until well-blended. Place over the stove and whisk the pastry cream continually over low heat until it begins to thicken.

2. Turn off heat immediately and add butter. Continue whisking until the melted butter blends in. Remove saucepan from the heat. Strain the mixture to get a silky smooth cream. Allow it to cool down before refrigerating for at least 2–3 hours.

3. Preheat the oven to 180°C (350°F) for at least 10–15 minutes. Grease a 26 x 13 cm (10 x 5 in) *tranche* (rectangular tray) with a loose-bottomed tray.

4. Prepare orange tart pastry. Place flour on a floured kitchen top. Make a well in the middle of the flour. Place the castor sugar, butter, salt, vanilla extract and orange zest. Crack an egg on top of the ingredients. Using a fork, swirl the ingredients into the flour and mix until it forms a dough. Sprinkle flour to prevent it from sticking to your fingers. Knead for 2 minutes until the dough becomes smooth and does not stick to your fingers.

5. Roll out the pastry between 2 silicon baking sheets to 3 mm (⅛ in) thickness. Peel off the top silicon sheet. Lift up the bottom sheet together with the pastry and flip it into the base of the tray. Press the dough against the base and sides of the tray until even. Using a fork, dock the bottom pastry by pricking the pastry a few times before baking.

6. Blind bake for 15 minutes. After removing the beans and parchment paper, continue baking for another 5 minutes until the pastry base is cooked. Set aside to cool down.

7. **To assemble:** Spoon the pastry cream over the base to about two-thirds full. Chill until the cream sets. Top with assorted cut fruits of your choice. Refrigerate.

8. Prepare glaze. Mix the jam and water with hot water in a small saucepan until well combined. Cook over low heat until it becomes a slightly sticky liquid. Using a pastry brush, coat the fruit with the glaze while it is still warm. Chill for 30 minutes before serving.

NOTE: Substitute orange tart pastry with a double portion of the chocolate pastry if desired.

# Coconut and Pineapple Tartlets

Makes about 30 tartlets

Pineapple and coconut ooze vibrant tropical aromas! This tart is a throwback to
the sixties when coconut tarts crowned with a red maraschino cherry were considered a treat.
Sarah's inspiration for this tart came from a café bakery in her hometown
popular for its coconut and pineapple confection.

30 store-bought sweet shortcrust
tartlet cases

**COCONUT FILLING**

10 g sugar

50 ml (1²/₃ fl oz) water

1 pandan leaf, knotted

80 g (2⁴/₅ oz) freshly grated
skinned coconut

¹/₂ tsp salt

**PINEAPPLE JAM**

1 large pineapple, peeled, cored
and coarsely chopped

125 g (4¹/₂ oz) sugar

2 cloves

2 cm (³/₄ in) cinnamon stick

1 tsp lemon juice

1. Prepare coconut filling. In a small saucepan, boil sugar and water with the pandan leaf over medium heat until the sugar has dissolved. Add grated coconut and salt. Cook for 5 minutes. Remove from the heat, discard pandan leaf. Allow it to cool.

2. Prepare pineapple jam. Place grated pineapple, sugar, cloves, and cinnamon into a small saucepan and cook over low heat until it turns into a thick and gooey paste with a jam-like consistency. Remove from the heat and add lemon juice. Mix well. Allow it to cool.

3. Preheat oven to 180°C (350°F) for 10–15 minutes.

4. **To assemble:** Fill half of each tartlet case with half teaspoon of pineapple jam followed by 1 heaped teaspoon coconut filling. Repeat until both fillings are used up.

5. Bake until the coconut turns slightly brown or until a buttery aroma fills the air.

*Tip* Store-bought tartlet cases
are available at baking supply shops.
Prepare the coconut filling and
pineapple jam a few days ahead.

# Thai Pumpkin Custard Tart

*Makes one 23-cm (9-in) tart*

We adapted the much-adored Thai dessert, *sankaya*, into this appetising tart
that comprises an additional element — firm pastry that holds up the delicious
coconut-flavoured egg custard which cushions buttery orangey pumpkin.

1 egg white, lightly beaten

**PASTRY**

225 g (8 oz) plain (all-purpose) flour

150 g (5 oz) ground almond

180 g (6 oz) butter, chilled

50 g (1²/₃ oz) sugar

A pinch of salt

1 egg yolk

**CUSTARD**

4 eggs

2 egg yolks

250 ml (8 fl oz / 1 cup) coconut cream
(*santan pekat*)

50 g (1²/₃ oz) Thai coconut palm sugar,
grated

A pinch of salt

600 g (1 lb 5¹/₃ oz) pumpkin, cut into
5-mm (¹/₅-in) thick slices, skin on

> *Tip* Always use fresh coconut
> milk or cream. Do not freeze it as
> the solids in the milk/cream will
> separate from the water.

1. Make pastry base 1 day ahead. Prepare pastry. Place all ingredients except for egg yolk in a food processor and pulse until it comes together. Add the egg yolk and continue to pulse until it forms a dough. Remove, knead into a disc and wrap with cling film and refrigerate for 30 minutes. If making the dough on baking day, blast chill by putting it in a freezer for at least 15 minutes.

2. Preheat oven to 180°C (350°C) for at least 10–15 minutes.

3. **To assemble:** Roll the dough out between 2 silicon baking sheets or onto a lightly floured surface to a 3 mm (¹/₈ in) thickness, with about 5 cm (2 in) in excess of the base. Dock the bottom pastry using a fork to prick the base. Brush tart base with egg white.

4. Blind bake for 15 minutes using parchment paper and beans. Remove beans. Bake for another 5 minutes until the bottom pastry is cooked.

5. Prepare custard. In a mixing bowl, beat eggs and egg yolks with coconut cream, grated Thai coconut palm sugar and salt until well mixed.

6. Steam pumpkin for 5 minutes until it softens. This makes it easier to line the pumpkin slices inside the tray.

7. Line the tart with pumpkin slices in concentric circles starting with the outer circumference and working towards the centre. Pour in the custard mixture. Bake for 75 minutes.

8. Allow the tart to cool down before serving.

# Sweetcorn Ice Cream Pie

Makes: 6 individual portions in champagne glasses

Sweetcorn ice cream sandwiched between sliced bread
was one of Sarah's many childhood indulgences. She would eagerly anticipate
the ice cream man cruising the neighbourhood for her sweet treat.
This dessert is about reliving those finger-licking memories!

6 champagne glasses

**PASTRY BASE**
55 g (2 oz) walnuts
55 g (2 oz) desiccated coconut
55 g (2 oz) ground almonds
2 Tbsp virgin coconut oil
$^1/_2$ Tbsp honey
A pinch of salt
1 Tbsp water

**FILLING**
Sweetcorn ice cream

**TOPPING**
Whipped cream
Store-bought granola

1. Prepare pastry base. Place walnuts in a spice grinder and grind until fine. Transfer to a medium mixing bowl. Mix in the desiccated coconut and ground almonds. Using a mixer, grind until the coconut is fairly fine. Add coconut oil, honey and a pinch of salt. Add water and mix to a dough.

2. **To assemble**: Press dough firmly onto the base of each glass to form a crust. Chill until it sets. Spoon slightly softened ice cream over the pastry until two-thirds filled. Repeat until both pastry and ice cream have been filled into the glasses. Place them on a tray and into the freezer overnight.

3. Top with whipped cream and serve with a sprinkle of granola.

# Red Bean and Pulot Hitam Tartlets

Makes 50 tartlets

Red beans and black glutinous rice are simmered in fragrant coconut milk
sweetened with palm sugar to a fairly gooey paste. The flavour profile
hint of caramel, vanilla, nutty and floral.

45–50 store-bought 5.5 x 2 cm
  (2$^1$/$_4$ x $^3$/$_4$ in) shortcrust tartlet cases

## FILLING

100 g (3$^1$/$_2$ oz) red beans, soaked
  for 30 minutes

85 g (3 oz) black glutinous rice
  (*pulot hitam*), soaked overnight

1 Tbsp white rice, uncooked

2 pandan leaves

1$^1$/$_2$ litres (48 fl oz / 6 cups) water

125 g (4$^1$/$_2$ oz) palm sugar
  (*gula melaka*)

125 ml (4 fl oz / $^1$/$_2$ cup) coconut cream
  (*santan pekat*) + 1 tsp salt

1 Tbsp sago pearls

## COCONUT CREAM TOPPING

60 ml (2 fl oz / $^1$/$_4$ cup) coconut cream
  (*santan pekat*)

 1 Tbsp sugar

$^1$/$_4$ tsp salt

$^1$/$_2$ tsp cornstarch

*Tip* Do not wash the sago
pearls before adding into the
bean mixture.

1. Prepare filling. Place red beans, black glutinous rice, white rice, pandan
   leaves and water in a medium saucepan and cook over medium heat for
   about 1.5 hours until beans are soft and the mixture thickens.

2. Add palm sugar. Reduce heat to a simmer, add coconut cream and mix
   well. Cook for 20 minutes, then sprinkle the sago pearls over the bean
   mixture, stirring continuously. Simmer for another 15 minutes and then
   turn off heat. The sago pearls will still have a white heart and will
   continue to cook in the residual heat. Allow filling to cool down overnight.

3. Preheat oven to 180°C (350°F) for at least 10–15 minutes.

4. Heat up the pastry cases for 10 minutes in the oven until the buttery
   aroma of the pastry wafts in the air. Remove and allow them to cool.

5. **To assemble:** Using a teaspoon, fill each pastry case up to the brim with
   the filling.

6. Prepare coconut cream topping. Place all ingredients in a small saucepan
   over low heat and cook for 3 minutes until it begins to thicken. Drizzle in
   the coconut cream and swirl it in.

# Glossary

**❶ Galangal (*Lengkuas*)**
Galangal is a rhizome that resembles ginger but has a compact and dense texture, which makes it woody when mature. It is touted for its medicinal and culinary uses, especially in spice pastes (*rempah*) for curries, marinades, soups and sauces. Fresh galangal is best — it is gingery with peppery nuances, and also has a lemony scent and even pine notes. Galangal is commonly used bruised (with a cleaver or mortar and pestle), sliced or ground to a powder/paste.

**❷ Kaffir Lime Leaves (*Daun Limau Purut*)**
Kaffir lime leaves are used more so than the fruit. Many signature Thai, Malaysian and Indonesian recipes call for kaffir lime leaves for an infusion of citrusy flavours. The young leaves with the centre spines removed are shredded thinly for *nasi ulam* or rice salads, added to *sambal belacan* and even in desserts like *kueh-mueh*, cakes and cookies. The larger mature leaves are tossed into stir-fries, curries and soups like tom yam. The knobbly, wrinkly and thick rind of the fruit is also used in curries.

**❸ Lemongrass (*Serai*)**
Lemongrass tastes and smells like sun-ripened lemons releasing citrusy aromas when squeezed. It also has grassy, floral notes with hints of mint and ginger. It is commonly served as a tea and also added to soups, curries, and stews. Lemongrass is also ideal for poultry, seafood and meat (pork, beef) and lends an exotic rose and floral fragrance to dishes it is cooked with. Lemongrass is predominantly used in Malaysian, Thai, Indonesian, Vietnamese cooking especially the savoury and sweet dishes.

**❹ Stink Beans (*Petai*)**
*Petai*, because of its pervasive pungent odour, is nicknamed stink beans because of the characteristic strong odour it emits after ingestion. Barring its odour, *petai* is high in dietary fibre that helps to keep the digestive system healthy. In actual fact, they are not beans but seeds of the tall rainforest tree that grows in tropical climates of Indonesia, Malaysia, Thailand and Philippines.

**❺ Thai Basil Leaf**
Thai basil is a fresh herb frequently used in Thai and Vietnamese cuisines. Usually eaten raw as an accompaniment to *pho* (soup noodles with either chicken or beef) the delicate purple-veined leaves, which are slightly spicy, possess anise and licorice aromas. It is used to flavour Thai green and red curries or cooked with minced meat or poultry in stir-fries.

**❻ Torch Ginger Bud (*Bunga Kantan*)**
Torch ginger flower or *bunga kantan* is an indispensable ingredient in *rojak* (fruit and vegetable salad in a spicy prawn paste dressing) and also adds complexity to Penang *asam* laksa, a spicy noodle soup with fish flakes. Due to its pungent flavour, it is able to mask fishy odour and zest up seafood stews.

**❼ Turmeric (*Kunyit*)**
Turmeric is more often used fresh than in its other forms — powdered or dried. It is one of the primary ingredients in the Asian spice pantry. A deep mustard colour, turmeric gives a pleasing mild fragrance that hints of orange and ginger with warm peppery undertones. Its light green aromatic leaves add a distinctive flavour to curries in Indian, Malaysian and Thai cooking. Always buy leaves that are fresh and avoid using the wilted ones. When used dried, soak the leaves in water and use the extract for cooking.

**❽ Vietnamese Mint**
This is also known as laksa leaves in Malaysia and Singapore as it is used as a garnish in laksa (rice noodles cooked in spicy coconut milk based soup). It is also eaten raw in salads. The fresh dark green leaves have hints of cilantro, citrus and mint. Although it is called Vietnamese mint, it is closer to the coriander plant than the mint family.

**❾ Wild Pepper Leaves**
This herb belonging to the pepper family is commonly found in Southeast Asia. It is also known as *cha plu* in Thai. In Malaysia, the leaves are used in making Penang *otah* whereas in Thailand, the Thais eat them raw in a salad with dried shrimps, roasted peanuts, diced shallots, ginger, toasted coconut among others.

**⑩ Candied Winter Melon (*Dong Gua*)**

Often used fresh, winter melon is a succulent white-fleshed vegetable cooked in soups, braised items and stir-fries in Chinese cooking. It is also used as a filling for Asian pastries such as lao po or sweetheart cake that is popular in Hong Kong and *hopia*, a Filipino snack that originated from Fujian.

**⑪ Candlenuts (*Buah Keras*)**

Candlenuts are usually ground before cooking and become creamy when mixed with water. It is used to thicken curries or satay sauce in Malaysian and Indonesian curries. Known as *kemiri* in Indonesian or *buah keras* in Malay, the candlenuts have a waxy texture. Good substitutes include the macadamia, cashew nut or Brazil nut which have a similar creamy consistency when ground.

**⑫ Cinnamon Stick (*Kayu Manis*)**

Cinnamon or *kayu manis* as it is called in Malay has warm earthy flavours with a pleasing sweet aroma. It is applauded for its versatility in flavouring both savoury and sweet dishes such as stews, curries, sauces, fruits, desserts, beverages and baked goods in both Asian and Western cooking. The bark is harvested during the rainy season when it is pliable and then dried until they get their characteristic curls. It is also sold in powder form.

**⑬ Cloves (*Cengkih*)**

Cloves are native trees grown in eastern Indonesia with pink flower buds that are hand-picked and sun-dried until toasty brown. They may be small but have an intense spice aroma. Use the ground spice sparingly to avoid overpowering the dish.

**⑭ Dried Shrimp Paste (*Belacan*)**

Compact dried shrimp paste or *belacan* as it is called in Malay or terasi in Indonesian is made from fermented baby shrimps cured in salt, then sun-dried and sold in discs or rectangular blocks. These days, the dried powdered version is readily available in supermarkets. It is used in sambals, curries and in sambal *belacan*, a chilli shrimp paste condiment, eaten as a dip in Peranakan cooking.

**⑮ Indonesian Black Nuts (*Buah Keluak*)**

The kernels of *buah keluak,* an Indonesian black nut, are used in Peranakan and Indonesian cuisines. The nuts need to be soaked several days before cooking to rid them of hydrocyanic acid, a poisonous substance; the black kernel meat (hence its name black nuts) is then extracted and seasoned with salt. It is either mixed with minced pork/chicken/prawns or left on its own before it is stuffed back into the empty shells. An acquired taste, the pure kernel meat hints of a blend of mushrooms, black olive and cacao. Its unique flavour gives the signature Nyonya *ayam buah keluak* (chicken cooked with Indonesian black nuts) its characteristic taste.

**⑯ Nutmeg (*Buah Pala*)**

Nutmeg is a favoured spice in Asian and Middle Eastern cuisines. The whole seed is wrapped in a red lace known as mace, and is also used as a spice to add sweet-spicy flavours. It is processed in different ways and consumed in a variety of dishes. The brown seed itself, when cracked is used in cooking soups like Penang *itek tim* (duck soup with salted vegetables), Indonesian *sup buntut* (oxtail soup), Indian *sup kambing* (mutton soup) and even in Japanese curries.

**⑰ Star Anise (*Bunga Lawang*)**

The star-shaped seed pod with eight segments has licorice flavours. Not to be confused with anise seeds, this spice with its sweet herbal accents is far more potent and alluring. It works well for baked and chilled desserts especially pear and apple as it infuses the fruit with a heady spice aroma. Star anise should be used sparingly as it is potent and sometimes a segment or two suffices as using the entire star might overwhelm the food, causing it to be bitter.

**⑱ Tamarind Peel (*Asam Keping*)**

Tamarind peels are a cross-section of a yellow pumpkin-coloured fruit, *asam gelugur* is that resembles an orange mangosteen. It is used as a souring agent in dishes like Penang *asam* laksa, curries and rendang. This is more sour than *asam jawa* or tamarind paste. To prepare tamarind water — mix 1 tablespoon of pulp with 5 tablespoons of warm water using your fingers to extract 4 tablespoons of tamarind water. Discard the seeds and pulp.

**⑲ Cardamom (*Buah Pelaga*)**

Cardamom has a dominant, pungent flavour and is chiefly used to flavour curries, rice dishes like *nasi biryani*, desserts and even drinks especially in Indian cooking. With hints of lemon and mint, cardamom opens up the palate, adding a complexity to sweet and savoury dishes. Use with restrain as an overdose can add a herbal bitterness to dishes. They are sold in two different colours — the green ones (touted as the real McCoy) which are picked in their prime and hence more intense and the black ones with its larger pods which have a smoky flavour because they are dried over a fire pit.

**⑳ Coriander (*Ketumbar*)**

Coriander is the dried seed of cilantro. In its raw form, it has earthy scents that releases a cinnamon aroma with citrusy scents when freshly toasted. When ground, the flavour profile of the spice becomes irresistibly appealing — aromatic, buttery and nutty with hints of cinnamon. Food that is cooked with ground coriander in particular takes on a warm lemony lilt that lingers on the palate.

**㉑ Cumin (*Jintan Putih*)**

Cumin is a key ingredient in curry powders used in Asian cooking. The pale green oval dried fruit of the parsley has a distinctively bitter taste that leaves a tinge of warmth on the tongue. Cumin imparts robust flavours to simple ingredients from poultry, meat, legumes and vegetables to rice and potatoes.

**㉒ Fennel (*Jintan Manis*)**

Fennel looks similar to cumin; the yellowish-green oval dried fruit actually comes from the fennel plant known for its licorice flavours. To extract its aniseed flavours, they are toasted and then ground to a powder. It is often served as an "after-dinner mint" at the end of an Indian meal paired with cubed sugar primarily to freshen the breath when chewed as well as to aid digestion.

**㉓ Fenugreek Leaves**

The leaves, available fresh or dried, are used as a herb and a spice in curries and stews.

**㉔ Five-spice Powder**

Five-spice powder, commonly used in Chinese cooking, is a blend of basic spices that include cinnamon, Szechuan peppercorns, star anise, fennel and clove. The combination may even include ginger and white/black pepper. Contrary to common perception, the numeric 5 does not refer to the number of spices but actually refers to the flavour profiles that characterise Chinese cuisine — sweet, salty, sour, bitter and spicy. Five-spice is perfect for tempering strong flavoured, gamey, fatty meats such as duck, venison and wild boar.

**㉕ Mustard Seed (*Biji Sawi*)**

The small, round seeds of the mustard plant are often used in Indian cooking either during stir-fries or in curries. Although mustard seeds are commonly sold as black seeds, they come in shades of yellowish white to brown and black. The seeds are usually tossed into hot oil to allow them to pop so as to release its distinctively pungent flavours of hot and spicy. Mustard seeds are a good complement to dishes with cabbage, beef and poultry.

**㉖ Salted Bean Paste (*Salted Taucheo*), Sweet Bean Paste (*Sweet Taucheo*)**

Fermented bean paste, made from ground soybeans, comes in two types: salted and a sweeter version which is less salty. The colour, depending on the production method can range from light to reddish and dark brown owing to the addition of ingredients at different stages like wheat flour, rice or sugar or even the presence of microflora. The salted version is used in stir-fries and stews e.g. Nyonya *chap chye* (Nyonya vegetarian dish), Nyonya *babi/ayam ponteh* (pork or chicken stew with Chinese mushrooms) or for steamed fish with ginger.

**Shaoxing Rice Wine**

Shaoxing wine is a traditional Chinese yellow wine fermented from glutinous rice, wheat and water. It got its name from Shao Xing, a city in China. The amber-coloured fragrant wine, with mushroomy notes, is a standard spirit used in Chinese cooking. Usually homemade in China, there's a tradition where jugs of wine buried in the ground when a daughter is born is served on her wedding day. It is also interchangeably called *Hua Diao* wine. Shaoxing wine can be substituted with mirin (Japanese rice wine) or dry sherry.

# Weights & Measures

Quantities for this book are given in Metric and American (spoon and cup) measures. Standard spoon and cup measurements used are: 1 tsp = 5 ml, 1 Tbsp = 15 ml, 1 cup = 250 ml. All measures are level unless otherwise stated.

## LIQUID AND VOLUME MEASURES

| Metric | Imperial | American |
|---|---|---|
| 5 ml | $^1/_6$ fl oz | 1 teaspoon |
| 10 ml | $^1/_3$ fl oz | 1 dessertspoon |
| 15 ml | $^1/_2$ fl oz | 1 tablespoon |
| 60 ml | 2 fl oz | $^1/_4$ cup (4 tablespoons) |
| 85 ml | $2^1/_2$ fl oz | $^1/_3$ cup |
| 90 ml | 3 fl oz | $^3/_8$ cup (6 tablespoons) |
| 125 ml | 4 fl oz | $^1/_2$ cup |
| 180 ml | 6 fl oz | $^3/_4$ cup |
| 250 ml | 8 fl oz | 1 cup |
| 300 ml | 10 fl oz ($^1/_2$ pint) | $1^1/_4$ cups |
| 375 ml | 12 fl oz | $1^1/_2$ cups |
| 435 ml | 14 fl oz | $1^3/_4$ cups |
| 500 ml | 16 fl oz | 2 cups |
| 625 ml | 20 fl oz (1 pint) | $2^1/_2$ cups |
| 750 ml | 24 fl oz ($1^1/_5$ pints) | 3 cups |
| 1 litre | 32 fl oz ($1^3/_5$ pints) | 4 cups |
| 1.25 litres | 40 fl oz (2 pints) | 5 cups |
| 1.5 litres | 48 fl oz ($2^2/_5$ pints) | 6 cups |
| 2.5 litres | 80 fl oz (4 pints) | 10 cups |

## DRY MEASURES

| Metric | Imperial |
|---|---|
| 30 grams | 1 ounce |
| 45 grams | $1^1/_2$ ounces |
| 55 grams | 2 ounces |
| 70 grams | $2^1/_2$ ounces |
| 85 grams | 3 ounces |
| 100 grams | $3^1/_2$ ounces |
| 110 grams | 4 ounces |
| 125 grams | $4^1/_2$ ounces |
| 140 grams | 5 ounces |
| 280 grams | 10 ounces |
| 450 grams | 16 ounces (1 pound) |
| 500 grams | 1 pound, $1^1/_2$ ounces |
| 700 grams | $1^1/_2$ pounds |
| 800 grams | $1^3/_4$ pounds |
| 1 kilogram | 2 pounds, 3 ounces |
| 1.5 kilograms | 3 pounds, $4^1/_2$ ounces |
| 2 kilograms | 4 pounds, 6 ounces |

## LENGTH

| Metric | Imperial |
|---|---|
| 0.5 cm | $^1/_4$ inch |
| 1 cm | $^1/_2$ inch |
| 1.5 cm | $^3/_4$ inch |
| 2.5 cm | 1 inch |

## OVEN TEMPERATURE

| | °C | °F | Gas Regulo |
|---|---|---|---|
| Very slow | 120 | 250 | 1 |
| Slow | 150 | 300 | 2 |
| Moderately slow | 160 | 325 | 3 |
| Moderate | 180 | 350 | 4 |
| Moderately hot | 190/200 | 370/400 | 5/6 |
| Hot | 210/220 | 410/440 | 6/7 |
| Very hot | 230 | 450 | 8 |
| Super hot | 250/290 | 475/550 | 9/10 |

## ABBREVIATION

| | |
|---|---|
| tsp | teaspoon |
| Tbsp | tablespoon |
| g | gram |
| kg | kilogram |
| ml | millilitre |